LIVING WORDS

LIVING WORDS

Soul-Kindlers for the New Millennium

Gleanings from the Works of

SRI AUROBINDO

and

THE MOTHER

Compiled by

A. S. Dalal

SRI AUROBINDO ASHRAM
PONDICHERRY

First Edition: 2000
Reprinted: 2005

Rs. 60.00
ISBN 81-7058-588-0

Published by Sri Aurobindo Ashram Publication Department,
Pondicherry - 605 002
Website: http://sabda.sriaurobindoashram.org
Printed at Sri Aurobindo Ashram Press, Pondicherry
PRINTED IN INDIA

CONTENTS

PREFACE

The idea of this compilation was suggested by the experience which one has in reading certain passages from the works of Sri Aurobindo and the Mother, or listening to certain recorded talks of the Mother, particularly the latter because of the additional effect of the sound vibrations. These writings and talks are felt as speaking not so much to the mind as to the soul. The words do not just convey certain ideas but also induce a psychic or soul state of consciousness. They are living words which are alive and vibrant with a consciousness that is greater than that of the mind. The words have the ring of the spirit and are capable of kindling the spirit when one is in a receptive state. Passages contained in the previous compilations by the same Editor have generally not been included in this book.

The great majority of extracts contained in this book have been selected because of the quality described above. However, some passages have been included more for their relevance to the message of the book. The central message of the book is that evolution — which is a progressive unfoldment of the Spirit through progressively higher levels of consciousness — has reached a stage where the next leap of consciousness is preparing to take place, the leap from mind to that which is beyond mind — the Supermind.

As plant-life contains in itself the obscure possibility of the conscious animal, as the animal-mind is astir with the movements of feeling and perception and the

> rudiments of conception that are the first ground for man the thinker, so man the mental being is sublimated by the endeavour of the evolutionary Energy to develop out of him the spiritual man, the fully conscious being, man exceeding his first material self and discoverer of his true self and highest nature.
>
> Sri Aurobindo, *The Life Divine*, p. 851

Man the mental being is thus a transitional creature, to be superceded by one whom Sri Aurobindo calls the supramental being or the fully spiritual man. The New Age, heralding the coming of the supramental being, has now dawned.

How long would it take for the arrival of the supramental being? Regarding the time it takes to evolve each succeeding level of consciousness from Matter to Supermind, Sri Aurobindo writes:

> The first obscure material movement of the evolutionary Force is marked by an aeonic graduality; the movement of life-progress proceeds slowly but still with a quicker step, it is concentrated into the figure of milleniums; mind can still further compress the tardy leisurelieness of Time and make long paces of the centuries; but when the conscious spirit intervenes, a supremely concentrated pace of evolutionary swiftness becomes possible.
>
> Sri Aurobindo, *The Life Divine*, p. 932

To give an idea of the quickened pace of evolution, the Mother states that whereas the evolution of the human brain from the animal brain (and the consequent emergence of man from the animal) took nearly a million years, we may expect the supramental race to succeed the human race "in a few centuries"[1]. She added that this time-frame applies to the appearance of the supramental *race*. So far as *individual* transformation is concerned, "the time has come when some beings among the *élite* of humanity, who fulfil the conditions necessary for supramentalisation, will be able to transform their bodies with the help of the supramental Force, Consciousness and Light so as no longer to be animal-men but become supermen."[2]

The conditions necessary for spiritualisation and the path to be followed by the individual are stated in the last pages of this book (pp. 189–92).

A. S. Dalal

[1] *Collected Works of the Mother*, Vol. 8, p. 323.

[2] *Ibid.*

Nothing can be taught to the mind which is not already concealed as potential knowledge in the unfolding soul of the creature. So also all perfection of which the outer man is capable, is only a realising of the eternal perfection of the Spirit within him. We know the Divine and become the Divine because we are That already in our secret nature. All teaching is a revealing, all becoming is an unfolding. Self-attainment is the secret; self-knowledge and an increasing consciousness are the means and the process.

The usual agency of this revealing is the Word, the thing heard (*śruta*). The Word may come to us from within; it may come to us from without. But in either case, it is only an agency for setting the hidden knowledge to work. The word within may be the utterance of the inmost soul in us which is always open to the Divine; or it may be the word of the secret and universal Teacher who is seated in the hearts of all. There are rare cases in which none other is needed, for all the rest of the Yoga is an unfolding under that constant touch and guidance; the lotus of the knowledge discloses itself from within by the power of irradiating effulgence which proceeds from the Dweller in the lotus of the heart. Great

indeed, but few are those to whom self-knowledge from within is thus sufficient and who do not need to pass under the dominant influence of a written book or a living teacher.

Ordinarily, the Word from without, representative of the Divine, is needed as an aid in the work of self-unfolding; and it may be either a word from the past or the more powerful word of the living Guru.

Sri Aurobindo, *The Synthesis of Yoga*, p. 48

A teaching can be profitable only if it is perfectly sincere, that is, if it is lived while it is being given, and words often repeated, thoughts expressed frequently can no longer be sincere.

The Mother, *Prayers and Meditations*, p. 56

1. LIVING WORDS

Living Question, Living Teaching

In fact, if one reads attentively what Sri Aurobindo has written, all that he has written, one would have the answer to every question. But there are certain moments and certain ways of presenting ideas which have a dynamic effect on the consciousness and help you to make a spiritual progress. The presentation, to be effective, must necessarily be the spontaneous expression of an immediate experience. If things which have already been said are repeated in the same manner, things which belong to past experiences, it becomes a sort of teaching, what could be called didactic talk, and it sets off some cells in the brain, but in fact is not very useful.

For me, for what I am trying to do, action in silence is *always* much more important.... The force which is at work is not limited by words, and this gives it an infinitely greater strength, and it expresses itself in each consciousness in accordance with its own particular mode, which makes it infinitely more effective. A certain vibration is given out in silence, with a special purpose, to obtain a definite result, but according to the mental receptivity of each person it is expressed in each individual consciousness exactly in the form which can be the most effective, the most active, the most immediately useful for each individual; while if it is formulated in words, this formula has to be received by each person in its fixity — the fixity of the words given to it — and it loses much of its strength and fullness of action because, first, the words are not always understood as they are said and then they are not always adapted to the understanding of each one.

So, unless a question immediately gives rise to an experience which can be expressed as a new formula, in my opinion it is always better to keep silent. Only when the question is living can it give rise to an experience which will be the occasion of a living teaching. And for a question to be alive, it must answer an inner need for progress, a spontaneous need to progress on some plane or other — on the mental plane is the most usual way, but if by chance it answers an inner aspiration, a problem one is tackling and wants to solve, then the question becomes interesting and living and truly useful, and it can give rise to a vision, a perception on a higher plane, an experience in the consciousness which can make the formula new so that it carries a new power for realisation.

Apart from such cases I always feel that it is much better not to say anything and that a few minutes of meditation are always more useful.[1]

THE MOTHER

Two Methods of Teaching

You must have noticed on several occasions that my way of talking to you is not always the same. I don't know if you are very sensitive to the difference, but for me it is quite considerable.... Sometimes, either because of something I have read* or for quite another reason — following

* The Mother often read out a passage at the beginning of a class. — Ed.

a question sometimes, but pretty rarely — it so happens that I have what is usually called an experience, but in fact it is simply entering into a certain state of consciousness and, once in that state of consciousness, describing it. In that case what is said passes through the mind, making use of it only as a "storehouse of words", it could be said; the Force, the Consciousness which is expressing itself passes through the individual mind and attracts by a kind of affinity the words needed for its expression. That is the true teaching, something one rarely finds in books — it may be in books, but one must be in that state of consciousness oneself to be able to discover it. But with the spoken word, the vibration of the sound transmits something at least of the experience, which, for all those who are sensitive, can become contagious.

In the second case, the question asked or the subject chosen is conveyed by the mind to the higher Consciousness, then the mind receives a reply and transmits it again through the word. This is what usually happens in all teachings, provided that the person who teaches has the ability to pass on the question to the higher Consciousness, which is not always the case.

I must say the second method does not interest me very much, and that very often when the question or the subject dealt with does not give me the possibility of entering into an interesting state of consciousness, I would infinitely prefer to keep silent than to speak; it is a sort of duty to be fulfilled which makes me speak.[2]

THE MOTHER

2. RISING ABOVE THE SUBHUMAN

The course of evolution proceeding from the vegetable to the animal, from the animal to the man, starts in the latter from the subhuman; he has to take up into him the animal and even the mineral and vegetable: they constitute his physical nature, they dominate his vitality, they have their hold upon his mentality. His proneness to many kinds of inertia, his readiness to vegetate, his attachment to the soil and clinging to his roots, to safe anchorages of all kinds, and on the other hand his nomadic and predatory impulses, his blind servility to custom and the rule of the pack, his mob-movements and openness to subconscious suggestions from the group-soul, his subjection to the yoke of rage and fear, his need of punishment and reliance on punishment, his inability to think and act for himself, his incapacity for true freedom, his distrust of novelty, his slowness to seize intelligently and assimilate, his downward propensity and earthward gaze, his vital and physical subjection to his heredity, all these and more are his heritage from the subhuman origins of his life and body and physical mind. It is because of this heritage that he finds self-exceeding the most difficult of lessons and the most painful of endeavours. Yet it is by exceeding of the lower self that Nature accomplishes the great strides of her evolutionary process. To learn by what he has been, but also to know and increase to what he can be, is the task that is set for the mental being.[3]

SRI AUROBINDO

Much Needed to Come Out of the Animal

... the only thing which is very important for the moment is the change of consciousness. And don't think that this is so easy. If you observe yourself attentively, you will perceive that you think, feel, experience and construct like a human animal, that is, like an infrarational being who is three-fourths subconscious, through almost the whole of your day. It is possible that at certain moments you escape from this; but you still need an effort to escape from it. It may happen spontaneously, as by grace, at certain moments; but most of the time you have to make an effort to be able to catch something which is not purely this. At any time whatever of your day, if you take just a small step backwards and observe yourself, you will catch yourself, you will see that. When is it that... suddenly, you see, if I said all of a sudden, here, now, "Look at yourself!" like that, without warning you beforehand, what was it, there in the field of your consciousness? If you catch that, you will see; certainly at least ninety-nine times out of a hundred, it is the animal that's there; an animal which is a little improved, you know, not altogether a dog, not altogether a monkey, but still not very far from that.

There are many things which men have transformed into marvellous virtues, which I have found in animals as spontaneous movements — and they at least have the advantage of not being proud and not having any vanity. They did things spontaneously which, surely, were very remarkable — very remarkable in devotion, abnegation, foresight, educative sense. They did them spontaneously and without writing books on them and boasting about them as something marvellous. Therefore much is needed to come out of the animal, much more than one would think.[4]

THE MOTHER

Living Uselessly

That is the attitude of men in general: they come into life, they don't know why; they know that they will live a certain number of years, they don't know why; they think that they will have to pass away because everybody passes away, and they again don't know why; and then, most of the time they are bored because they have nothing in themselves, they are empty beings and there is nothing more boring than emptiness; and so they try to fill this by distraction, they become absolutely useless, and when they reach the end they have wasted their whole existence, all their possibilities — and everything is lost. This you will see: take a thousand men, out of them at least nine hundred and ninety are in this condition. It happens that they are born in certain circumstances or certain others, and they try, you see, to pass their time as well as they can, to be bored as little as possible, to suffer as little as possible, to have as good a time as possible; and everything is dull, lifeless, useless, stupid, and absolutely without any result. There, then. This is the majority of human beings, and they don't even think... they don't even ask themselves, "But indeed, why am I here? Why is there an earth? Why are there men? Why do I live?" No, all these things are absolutely uninteresting. The only interesting thing is to try to eat well, to have good fun, be nicely distracted, well married, have children, earn money and have all the advantages one can get from the point of view of desires, and above all, above all not think, not reflect, not ask any questions, and avoid all trouble. Yes, and then get out of it like that, without too many catastrophes. This is the general condition; this is what men call being reasonable. And in this way the world can turn round indefinitely for eternity, it will never progress. And this is why all these are like ants; they come, crawl, die, go away, come back, crawl again, die again, and so on. And it can last for eternities like this. Fortunately there are some who do the work of all the others, but it's only these who will make everything change one day.

So the first problem is to know on which side one wants to be: on the side of those who are doing something or the side of those who do nothing; on the side of those who, perhaps, will be able to understand what life is and do what is necessary for this life to culminate in something, or else of those who hardly care to understand anything at all and try to pass their time in having as few botherations as possible. Above all, no botherations!

There we are. This is the first choice. After this there are many others.[5]

THE MOTHER

3. ASCENSION BEYOND THE HUMAN

Man A Transitional Being

Man is a transitional being, he is not final; for in him and high beyond him ascend the radiant degrees which climb to a divine supermanhood.

The step from man towards superman is the next approaching achievement in the earth's evolution. There lies our destiny and the liberating key to our aspiring, but troubled and limited human existence — inevitable because it is at once the intention of the inner Spirit and the logic of Nature's process.

The appearance of a human possibility in a material and animal world was the first glint of a coming divine Light, — the first far-off intimation of a godhead to be born out of Matter. The appearance of the superman in the human world will be the fulfilment of that distant shining promise.

The difference between man and superman will be the difference between mind and a consciousness as far beyond it as thinking mind is beyond the consciousness of plant and animal; the differentiating essence of man is mind, the differentiating essence of superman will be supermind or a divine gnosis.

Man is a mind imprisoned, obscured and circumscribed in a precarious and imperfect living but imperfectly conscious body. The superman will be a supramental spirit which will envelop and freely use a conscious body, plastic to spiritual forces. His physical frame will be a firm support and an adequate radiant instrument for the spirit's divine play and work in Matter.

Mind, even free and in its own unmixed and unhampered element, is not the highest possibility of consciousness; for mind is not in possession of Truth, but only a minor vessel or an instrument and here an ignorant seeker plucking eagerly at a mass of falsehoods and half-truths for the unsatisfying pabulum of its hunger. Beyond mind is a supramental or gnostic power of consciousness that is in eternal possession of Truth; all its motion and feeling and sense and outcome are instinct and luminous with the inmost reality of things and express nothing else.

Supermind or gnosis is in its original nature at once and in the same movement an infinite wisdom and an infinite will. At its source it is the dynamic consciousness of the divine Knower and Creator.

When in the process of unfolding of an always greater force of the one Existence, some delegation of this power shall descend into our limited human nature, then and then only can man exceed himself and know divinely and divinely act and create; he will have become at last a conscious portion of the Eternal. The superman will be born, not a magnified mental being, but a supramental power descended here into a new life of the transformed terrestrial body. A gnostic supermanhood is the next distinct and triumphant victory to be won by the spirit descended into earthly nature.

The disk of a secret sun of Power and Joy and Knowledge is emerging out of the material consciousness in which our mind works as a chained slave or a baffled and impotent demiurge; supermind will be the formed body of that radiant effulgence.

Superman is not man climbed to his own natural zenith, not a superior degree of human greatness, knowledge, power, intelligence, will, character, genius, dynamic force, saintliness, love, purity or perfection. Supermind is something beyond mental man and his limits, a greater consciousness than the highest consciousness proper to human nature.

Man is a being from the mental worlds whose mentality works here involved, obscure and degraded in a physical brain, shut off from its own divinest powers and impotent to change life beyond certain narrow and precarious limits. Even in the highest of his kind it is baulked of its luminous possibilities of supreme force and freedom by this dependence. Most often and in most men it is only a servitor, a purveyor of amusements, a caterer of needs and interests to the life and the body. But the superman will be a gnostic king of Nature; supermind in him even in its evolutionary beginnings will appear as a ray of the eternal omniscience and omnipotence. Sovereign and irresistible it will lay hands on the mental and physical instruments, and, standing above and yet penetrating and possessing our lower already manifested parts, it will transform mind, life and body into its own divine and luminous nature.

Man in himself is hardly better than an ambitious nothing. He is a narrowness that reaches towards ungrasped widenesses, a littleness straining towards grandeurs which are beyond him, a dwarf enamoured of the heights. His mind is a darkened ray in the splendours of the universal Mind. His life is a striving exulting and suffering wave, an eager passion-tossed and sorrow-stricken or a blindly and dully toiling petty moment of the universal Life. His body is a labouring perishable speck in the material universe. An immortal soul is somewhere hidden within him and gives out from time to time some sparks of its presence, and an eternal spirit is above and overshadows with its wings and upholds with its power this soul continuity in his nature. But that greater spirit is obstructed from descent by the hard lid of his constructed personality and this inner radiant soul is wrapped, stifled and oppressed in dense outer coatings. In all but a few it is seldom active, in many hardly perceptible. The soul and spirit in man seem rather to exist above and behind his formed nature than to be a part of its visible reality; subliminal in his inner being or superconscient above in some unreached status, they are in his outer consciousness possibilities rather than things realised and present. The spirit is in course of birth rather than born in Matter.

This imperfect being with his hampered, confused, ill-ordered and mostly ineffective consciousness cannot be the end and highest height of the mysterious upward surge of Nature. There is something more that has yet to be brought down from above and is now seen only by broken glimpses through sudden rifts in the giant wall of our limitations. Or else there is something yet to be evolved from below, sleeping under the veil of man's mental consciousness or half visible by flashes, as life once slept in the stone and metal, mind in the plant and reason in the cave of animal memory underlying its imperfect apparatus of emotion and sense-device and instinct. Something there is in us yet unexpressed that has to be delivered by an enveloping illumination from above. A godhead is imprisoned in our depths, one in its being with a greater godhead ready to descend from superhuman summits. In that descent and awakened joining is the secret of our future.

Man's greatness is not in what he is but in what he makes possible. His glory is that he is the closed place and secret workshop of a living labour in which supermanhood is made ready by a divine Craftsman.

But he is admitted to a yet greater greatness and it is this that, unlike the lower creation, he is allowed to be partly the conscious artisan of his divine change. His free assent, his consecrated will and participation are needed that into his body may descend the glory that will replace him. His aspiration is earth's call to the supramental Creator.

If earth calls and the Supreme answers, the hour can be even now for that immense and glorious transformation.[6]

SRI AUROBINDO

The First Movement

> The process of Yoga is a turning of the human soul from the egoistic state of consciousness absorbed in the outward appearances... — *Sri Aurobindo*

I did not quite understand "the egoistic state of consciousness absorbed in the outward appearances..."

People are occupied with outward things. That means that the consciousness is turned towards external things — that is, all the things of life which one sees, knows, does — instead of being turned inwards in order to find the deeper truth, the divine Presence. This is the first movement. You are busy with all that you do, with the people around you, the things you use; and then with life: sleeping, eating, talking, working a little, having a little fun also; and then beginning over again: sleeping, eating, etc., etc., and then it begins again. And then what this one has said, what that one has done, what one ought to do, the lesson one ought to learn, the exercise one ought to prepare; and then again whether one is keeping well, whether one is feeling fit, etc. This is what one usually thinks about.

So the first movement — and it is not so easy — is to make all that pass to the background, and let one thing come inside and in front of the consciousness as *the* important thing: the discovery of the very purpose of existence and life, to learn what one is, why one lives, and what there is behind all this. This is the first step: to be interested more in the cause and goal than in the manifestation. That is, the first movement is a withdrawal of the consciousness from this total identification with outward and apparent things, and a kind of inward concentration on what one wants to discover, the Truth one wants to discover. This is the first movement.

Many people who are here forget one thing. They want to begin by the end. They think that they are ready to express in their life what they call the supramental Force or Consciousness, and they want to infuse this in their actions, their movements, their daily life. But the trouble is that they don't at all know what the supramental Force or Consciousness is and that first of all it is necessary to take the reverse path, the way of interiorisation and of withdrawal from life, in order to find within oneself this Truth which has to be expressed.

For as long as one has not found it, there is nothing to express. And by imagining that one is living an exceptional life, one lives only in the illusion of one's exceptional state. Therefore, at first not only must one find one's soul and the Divine who possesses it, but one must identify oneself with it. And then later, one may begin to come back to outward activities, and then transform them; because then one knows in what direction to turn them, into what to transform them.

One can't jump over this stage. One must first find one's soul, this is absolutely indispensable, and identify oneself with it. Later one can come to the transformation. Sri Aurobindo has written somewhere: "Our Yoga begins where the others end." Usually yoga leads precisely to this identification, this union with the Divine — that is why it is called "yoga". And when people reach this, well, they are at the end of their path and are satisfied. But Sri Aurobindo has written: we begin when they finish; you have found the Divine but instead of sitting down in contemplation and waiting for the Divine to take you out of your body which has become useless, on the contrary, with this consciousness you turn to the body and to life and begin the work of transformation — which is very hard labour. It's here that he compares it with cutting one's way through a virgin forest; because as nobody has done it before, one must make one's path where there was none. But to try to do this without having the indispensable directive of the union with the Divine within, within one's soul, is childishness.[7]

THE MOTHER

Interiorisation

Almost totally, everybody lives on the surface, all the time, all the time on the surface. And for them it's even the only thing which exists — the surface. And when something compels them to draw back from the surface, some people feel that they are falling into a hole. There are people who, if they are drawn back from the surface, suddenly feel that they are crumbling down into an abyss, so unconscious they are!

They are conscious only of a kind of small thin crust which is all that they know of themselves and things and the world, and it is so thin a crust! Many! I have experienced, I don't know how often... I tried to interiorise some people and immediately they felt that they were falling into an abyss, and at times a black abyss. Now this is the absolute inconscience. But a fall, a fall into something which for them is like a non-existence, this happens very often. People are told: "Sit down and try to be silent, to be very quiet"; this frightens them terribly.

A fairly long preparation is needed in order to feel an increase of life when one goes out of the outer consciousness. It is already a great progress. And then there is the culmination, that when one is obliged for some reason or other to return to the outer consciousness, it is there that one has the impression of falling into a black hole, at least into a kind of dull, lifeless greyness, a chaotic mixture of disorganised things, with the faintest light, and all this seems so dull, so dim, so dead that one wonders how it is possible to remain in this state — but this of course is the other end — unreal, false, confused, lifeless![8]

THE MOTHER

Learning to Look at Oneself

... when one thinks of "myself" one thinks of the body. That is the usual thing. The personal reality is the body's reality. It is only when one has made an effort for inner development and tried to find something that is a little more stable in one's being, that one can begin to feel that this "something" which is permanently conscious throughout all ages and all change, this something must be "myself". But that already requires a study that is rather deep. Otherwise if you think "I am going to do this", "I need that", it is always your body, a small kind of will which is a mixture of sensations, of more or less confused sentimental reactions, and still more confused thoughts which form a mixture and are animated by an impulse, an attraction, a desire, some sort of a will; and all that momentarily becomes "myself" — but not directly, for one does not conceive this "myself" as independent of the head, the trunk, the arms and legs and all that moves — it is very closely linked.

It is only after having thought much, seen much, studied much, observed much that you begin to realise that the one is more or less independent of the other and that the will behind can make it either act or not act, and you begin not to be completely identified with the movement, the action, the realisation — that something is floating. But you have to observe much to see that.

And then you must observe much more still to see that this, the second thing that is there, this kind of active conscious will, is set in motion by "something else" which watches, judges, decides and tries to found its decisions on knowledge — that happens even much later. And so, when you begin to see this "something else", you begin to see that it has the power to set in motion the second thing, which is an active will; and not only that, but that it has a very direct and very important action on the reactions, the feelings, the sensations, and that finally it can have control over all the movements of the being — this part which watches, observes, judges and decides.

That is the beginning of control.

When one becomes conscious of that, one has seized the thread, and when one speaks of control, one can know, "Ah! yes, this is what has the power of control."

This is how one learns to look at oneself.[9]

THE MOTHER

Individuality — the First Conquest

It is only gradually, very slowly, through the movements of life and a more or less careful and thorough education that you begin to have sensations which are personal to you, feelings and ideas which are personal to you. An individualised mind is something extremely rare, which comes only after a long education; otherwise it is a kind of thought-current passing through your brain and then through another's and then through a multitude of other brains, and all this is in perpetual movement and has no individuality. One thinks what others are thinking, others think what still others are thinking, and everybody thinks like that in a great mixture, because these are currents, vibrations of thought passing from one to another. If you look at yourself attentively, you will very quickly become aware that very few thoughts in you are personal. Where do you draw them from?—From what you have heard, from what you have read, what you have been taught, and how many of these thoughts you have are the result of your own experience, your own reflection, your purely personal observation?—Not many.

Only those who have an intense intellectual life, who are in the habit of reflecting, observing, putting ideas together, gradually form a mental individuality for themselves.

Most people—and not only those who are uneducated but even the well-read—can have the most contradictory, the most opposite ideas in their heads without even being aware of the contradictions. I have seen numerous examples like that, of people who cherished ideas and even had political, social, religious opinions on all the so-called higher fields of human intelligence, who had absolutely contradictory opinions on the same subject, and were not aware of it. And if you observe yourself, you will see that you have many ideas which ought to be linked by a sequence of intermediate ideas which are the result of a considerable widening of the thought if they are not to coexist in an absurd way.

... Some people, at a rather lower level, know themselves only by the name they bear. They would not be able to distinguish themselves from their neighbours except by their name. They are asked, "Who are you?"—"My name is this." A little later they tell you the name of their occupation or about their main characteristic. If they are asked, "Who are you?"—"I am a painter."

But at a certain level the only answer is the name. And what is a name? It is nothing but a word, isn't that so? And what is there behind? Nothing. It is a whole collection of vague things which do not at all represent a person as different from his neighbour. He is differentiated only because he has another name. If everybody bore the same name, it would be very difficult to distinguish one person from another!

... One lives by a kind of habit which is barely half-conscious — one lives, does not even objectify what one does, why one does it, how one does it. One does it by habit. All those who are born in a certain environment, a certain country, automatically take the habits of that environment, not only material habits but habits of thought, habits of feeling and habits of acting. They do it without watching themselves doing it, quite naturally, and if someone points this out to them they are astonished.

As a matter of fact, one has the habit of sleeping, speaking, eating, moving and one does all this as something quite natural, without wondering why or how.... And many other things. All the time one does things automatically, by force of habit, one does not watch oneself. And so, when one lives in a particular society, one automatically does what is normally done in that society. And if somebody begins to watch himself acting, watch himself feeling and thinking, he looks like a kind of phenomenal monster compared with the environment he lives in.

Therefore, individuality is not at all the rule, it is an exception, and if you do not have that sort of bag, a particular form which is your outer body and your appearance, you could hardly be distinguished from one another.

Individuality is a conquest. And... this first conquest is only a first stage, and once you have realised within you something like a personal independent and conscious being, then what you have to do is to break the form and go farther. For example, if you want to progress mentally, you must break all your mental forms, all your mental constructions to be able to make new ones. So, to begin with, a tremendous labour is required to individualise oneself, and afterwards one must demolish all that has been done in order to progress.[10]

THE MOTHER

The Three Victories

> For our entire nature and its environment, all our personal and all our universal self, are full of habits and of influences that are opposed to our spiritual rebirth...
>
> *Sri Aurobindo*

Our universal self is our relation with all others and all the movements of Nature.

... the first state of your being is a state of an almost total mixture with all things from outside, and that there is almost no individualisation, that is, specialisation which makes you a different being. You are moved — a kind of form which is your physical being is moved — by all the common universal forces, vital forces or mental forces, which go through your form and put it in motion.

So that is the universal being.

And all that you have wrested from this general semiconsciousness, and have crystallised into a more or less independent being, conscious of itself and having its own qualities, all this is your individual being. And this individual being is full of all the movements of obscurity, unconsciousness, and of the limitations of ordinary life, and that's... and that's what you must gradually open to the divine influence and bring to the consciousness and understanding of things. That's what Sri Aurobindo says.

In fact, the first victory is to create an individuality. And then later, the second victory is to give this individuality to the Divine. And the third victory is that the Divine changes your individuality into a divine being.

There are three stages: the first is to become an individual; the second is to consecrate the individual, that he may surrender entirely to the Divine and be identified with Him; and the third is that the Divine takes possession of this individual and changes him into a being in His own image, that is, he too becomes divine.

Generally, all the yogas stopped at the second. When one had succeeded in surrendering the individual and giving him without reserve to the Divine to be identified with Him, one considered that his work was finished, that all was accomplished.

But *we* begin there, and we say, "No, this is only a beginning. We want this Divine with whom we are identified to enter our individuality and make it into a divine personality acting in a divine world." And this is what we call transformation. But the other precedes it, must precede it. If that is not done, there is no possibility of doing the third. One can't go from the first to the third; one must pass through the second.[11]

THE MOTHER

To Be Thyself

It has been well said by one who saw but through a veil and mistook the veil for the face, that thy aim is to become thyself; and he said well again that the nature of man is to transcend himself. This is indeed his nature and that is indeed the divine aim of his self-transcending.

That which thou hast to transcend is the self that thou appearest to be, and that is man as thou knowest him, the apparent Purusha. And what is this man? He is a mental being enslaved to life and matter; and where he is not enslaved to life and matter, he is the slave of his mind. But this is a great and heavy servitude; for to be the slave of mind is to be the slave of the false, the limited and the apparent. The self that thou hast to become, is the self that thou art within behind the veil of mind and life and matter. It is to be the spiritual, the divine, the superman, the real Purusha. For that which is above the mental being, is the superman. It is to be the master of thy mind, thy life and thy body; it is to be a king over Nature of whom thou art now the tool, lifted above her who now has thee under her feet. It is to be free and not a slave, to be one and not divided, to be immortal and not obscured by death, to be full of light and not darkened, to be full of bliss and not the sport of grief and suffering, to be uplifted into power and not cast down into weakness. It is to live in the Infinite and possess the finite. It is to live in God and be one with him in his being. To become thyself is to be this and all that flows from it....

These things thou art, therefore thou canst become all this; but if thou wert not these things, then thou couldst never become them. What is within thee, that alone can be revealed in thy being. Thou appearest indeed to be other than this, but wherefore shouldst thou enslave thyself to appearances?

Rather arise, transcend thyself, become thyself. Thou art man and the whole nature of man is to become more than himself. He was the man-animal, he has become more than the animal man. He is the thinker, the craftsman, the seeker after beauty. He shall be more than the thinker, he shall be the seer of knowledge; he shall be more than the craftsman, he shall be the creator and master of his creation; he shall be more than the seeker of beauty, for he shall enjoy all beauty and all delight.[12]

SRI AUROBINDO

The True Goal

What happens most often when one makes the inner effort that's needed to discover one's soul, to unite with it and allow it to govern one's life, is a kind of marvellous enchantment with this discovery, as a result of which the first instinct is to tell oneself, "Now I have what I need, I have found infinite delight!" and no longer to be concerned with anything else.

In fact this is what has happened to almost all those who have made this discovery, and some of them have even set up this experience as a principle of realisation and said, "When you have done that, everything is done, there is nothing more to do; you have reached the goal and the end of the road."

Indeed, a great courage is necessary to go farther; this soul one discovers must be an intrepid warrior soul which does not at all rest satisfied with its own inner joy while comforting itself for the unhappiness of others with the idea that sooner or later everybody will reach that state and that it is good for others to make the same effort that one has made or, at best, that from this state of inner wisdom one can, with "great benevolence" and "deep compassion" help others to reach it, and that when everybody has attained it, well, that will be the end of the world and that's so much the better for those who don't like suffering!

But... there is a "but". Are you sure that this was the aim and intention of the Supreme when he manifested?

(*Silence*)

The whole creation, the whole universal manifestation appears at best like a very bad joke if it only comes to this. Why begin at all if it is only to get out of it! What is the use of having struggled so much, suffered so much, of having created something which, at least in its external appearance, is so tragic and dramatic, if it is simply to teach you how to get out of it — it would have been better not to begin at all.

But if one goes to the very depth of things, if, stripped not only of all egoism but also of the ego, one gives oneself totally, without reserve, so completely and disinterestedly that one becomes capable of understanding the plan of the Lord, then one knows that it is *not* a bad joke, *not* a tortuous path by which you return, a little battered, to the starting-point; on the contrary, it is to teach the entire creation the delight of being, the beauty of being, the greatness of being, the majesty of a sublime life, and the perpetual growth, perpetually progressive, of that delight, that beauty, that greatness. Then everything has a meaning, then one no longer regrets having struggled and suffered, one has only the enthusiasm to realise the divine goal, and one plunges headlong into the realisation with the *certitude* of the goal and victory.

But to know that, one must stop being egoistic, being a separate person turned in on oneself and cut off from the supreme origin. That is what must be done: to cast off one's ego. Then one can know the true goal — and this is the only way!

To cast off one's ego, to let it fall off like a useless garment.

The result is worth the efforts that must be made. And then, one is not all alone on the way. One is helped, if one has trust.

If you have had even a second's contact with the Grace — that marvellous Grace which carries you along, speeds you on the path, even makes you forget that you have to hurry — if you have had only a second's contact with that, then you can strive not to forget. And with the candour of a child, the simplicity of a child for whom there are no complications, give yourself to that Grace and let it do everything.

What is necessary is not to listen to what resists, not to believe what contradicts — to have trust, a real trust, a confidence which makes you give yourself fully without calculating, without bargaining. Trust! The trust that says, "Do this, do this for me, I leave it to You."

That is the best way.[13]

THE MOTHER

4. DESIRE, PAIN, PLEASURE AND DELIGHT

The Knot of Desire

In the path of works action is the knot we have first to loosen. —*Sri Aurobindo*

Why is action a knot?

Because one is attached to action. The knot is the knot of the ego. You act because of desire. Sri Aurobindo says this, doesn't he? The ordinary way of acting is tied to desire in one form or another — a desire, a need — so that is the knot. If you act only to satisfy desire — a desire which you call a need or a necessity or anything else, but in truth, if you go to the very root of the thing, you see that it is the impulse of a desire which makes you act — well, if you act only under the effect of the impulse of desire, you will no longer be able to act when you eliminate the desire.

And this is the first answer people give you. When they are told, "Act without being attached to the result of action, have this consciousness that it is not you who are acting, it is the Divine who is acting", the reply which ninety-nine and a half per cent give is, "But if I feel like that, I don't move any longer! I don't do anything any more; it is always a need, a desire, a personal impulse which makes me act in one way or another." So Sri Aurobindo says, if you want to realise this teaching of the Gita, the first thing to do is to loosen this knot, the knot binding action to desire — so firmly tied are they that if you take away one you take away the other. He says the knot must be loosened in order to be able to remove desire and yet continue to act.

And this is a fact, this is what must be done. The knot must be loosened. It is a small inner operation which you can very easily perform; and when it has been performed, you realise that you act absolutely without any personal motive, but moved by a Force higher than your egoistic force, and also more powerful. And then you act, but the consequences of action no longer return upon you.

This is a wonderful phenomenon of consciousness, and quite concrete. In life you do something — whatever you do, good, bad, indifferent, it doesn't matter — whatever it may be, it immediately has a series of consequences. In fact you do it to obtain a certain result, that is why you act, with an eye to the result. For example, if I stretch out my hand like this to take the mike, I am looking for the result, you see, to make sounds in the mike. And there is always a consequence, always. But if you loosen the knot and let a Force coming from above — or elsewhere — act through you and make you do things, though there are consequences of your action, they don't come to you any longer, for it was not you who initiated the action, it was the Force from above. And the consequences pass above, or else they are guided, willed, directed, controlled by the Force which made you act. And you feel *absolutely* free, nothing comes back to you of the result of what you have done.[14]

THE MOTHER

The Anguish of Desire

Where does desire come from?

The Buddha said that it comes from ignorance. It is more or less that. It is something in the being which fancies that it needs something else in order to be satisfied. And the proof that it is ignorance is that when one has satisfied it, one no longer cares for it, at least ninety-nine and a half times out of a hundred. I believe, right at its origin it is an obscure need for growth, as in the lowest forms of life love is changed into the need to swallow, absorb, become joined with another thing. This is the most primitive form of love in the lowest forms of life, it is to take and absorb. Well, the need to take is desire. So perhaps if we went back far enough into the last depths of the inconscience, we could say that the origin of desire is love. It is love in its obscurest and most unconscious form. It is a need to become joined with something, an attraction, a need to take, you see.

Take for instance... you see something which is — which seems to you or is — very beautiful, very harmonious, very pleasant; if you have the true consciousness, you experience this joy of seeing, of being in a conscious contact with something very beautiful, very harmonious, and then that's all. It stops there. You have the joy of it — that such a thing exists, you see. And this is quite common among artists who have a sense of beauty. For example, an artist may see a beautiful creature and have the joy of observing the beauty, grace, harmony of movement and all that, and that's all. It stops there. He is perfectly happy, perfectly satisfied, because he has seen something beautiful. An ordinary consciousness, altogether ordinary, dull like all ordinary consciousness — as soon as it sees something beautiful, whether it be an object or a person, hop! "I want it!" It is deplorable, you know. And into the bargain it doesn't even have the joy of the beauty, because it has the anguish of desire. It misses that and has nothing in exchange, because there is nothing pleasant in desiring anything. It only puts you in an unpleasant state, that's all.

The Buddha has said that there is a greater joy in overcoming a desire than in satisfying it. It is an experience everybody can have and one that is truly very interesting, very interesting.

There was someone who was invited — it happened in Paris — invited to a first-night (a first-night means a first performance) of an opera of Massenet's. I think... I don't remember now whose it was. The subject was fine, the play was fine, and the music not displeasing; it was the first time and this person was invited to the box of the Minister of Fine Arts who always has a box for all the first nights at the government theatres. This Minister of Fine Arts was a simple person, an old countryside man, who had not lived much in Paris, who was quite new in his ministry and took a truly childlike joy in seeing new things. Yet he was a polite man and as he had invited a lady he gave her the front seat and himself sat at the back. But he felt very unhappy because he could not see everything. He leaned forward like this, trying to see something without showing it too much. Now, the lady who was in front noticed this. She too was very interested and was finding it very fine, and it was not that she did not like it, she liked it very much and was enjoying the show; but she saw how very unhappy that poor minister looked, not being able to see. So quite casually, you see, she pushed back her chair, went back a little, as though she was thinking of something else, and drew back so well that he came forward and could now see the whole scene. Well, this person, when she drew back and gave up all desire to see the show, was filled with a sense of inner joy, a liberation from all attachment to things and a kind of peace, content to have done something for somebody instead of having satisfied herself, to the extent that the evening brought her infinitely greater pleasure than if she had listened to the opera. This is a true experience, it is not a little story read in a book, and it was precisely at the time this person was studying Buddhist discipline, and it was in conformity with the saying of the Buddha that she tried this experiment.

And truly this was so concrete an experience, you know, so real that... ah, two seconds later, you see, the play, the music, the actors, the scene, the pictures and all that were gone like absolutely secondary things, completely unimportant, while this joy of having mastered something in oneself and done something not simply selfish, this joy filled all the being with an incomparable serenity — a delightful experience... Well, it is not just an individual, personal experience. All those who want to try can have it.

There is a kind of inner communion with the psychic being which takes place when one willingly gives up a desire, and because of this one feels a much greater joy than if he had satisfied his desire. Besides, most usually, almost without exception, when one satisfies a desire it always leaves a kind of bitter taste somewhere.

There is not one satisfied desire which does not give

a kind of bitterness; as when one has eaten too sugary a sweet it fills your mouth with bitterness. It is like that. You must try sincerely. Naturally you must not pretend to give up desire and keep it in a corner, because then one becomes very unhappy. You must do it sincerely.[15]

THE MOTHER

Renunciation — Passage to Freedom

> All renunciation is for a greater joy yet ungrasped. Some renounce for the joy of duty done, some for the joy of peace, some for the joy of God and some for the joy of self-torture, but renounce rather as a passage to the freedom and untroubled rapture beyond.
>
> *Sri Aurobindo*

I have rarely had this experience of renunciation — for there to be renunciation, one must be attached to things, and there was always this thirst, this need to go further, to go higher, to feel better, to do better, to have something better. And rather than having a feeling of renunciation one has the feeling that it is a good riddance — you get rid of something cumbersome that weighs you down and hinders your advance. That is what I was saying the other day: we are still everything we no longer want to be and He is everything we want to become — what we call "we" in our egoistic stupidity is precisely what we do not want to be any more, and we would be so happy to throw all that off, to get rid of all that, so as to be able to be what we want to be.

This is a very living experience.

The only process that I have known, and which has been repeated several times during my life, is the renunciation of an error: something you believe to be true — which probably was true for a time — on which you base part of your action, but which in fact was only an opinion. You thought that it was a true evaluation with all its logical consequences, and your action — part of your action — was based on that, and it all followed automatically; and suddenly, an experience, a circumstance or an intuition, warns you that your evaluation is not as true as it looked. Then there is a whole period of observation, of study — or sometimes it comes like a revelation, a massive demonstration — and not only the idea or the false knowledge, but all its consequences must be changed — perhaps a whole way of acting on some point. And at that moment there is a kind of sensation, something akin to the sensation of renunciation, which means that you must break up a whole set of things which had been built — sometimes it can be quite extensive, sometimes it is something very small, but the experience is the same: it is the movement of a force, a power that dissolves, and there is resistance from everything which has to be dissolved, from all the past habits; and it is this movement of dissolution, with its corresponding resistance, which is probably expressed in the ordinary human consciousness as a feeling of renunciation.

I saw this very recently — it is insignificant, these circumstances have no importance in themselves; they are interesting only in the context of the study. This is the only phenomenon that is familiar to me because it has been repeated several times in my life. As the being progresses, the power of dissolution increases, becomes more and more immediate and the resistance diminishes. But I have the memory of a period of maximum resistance — it was more than half a century ago — and it was nothing but that, it was always something outside myself — not outside my consciousness, but outside my will — something which resisted the will. I have never had the feeling of having to renounce anything, but I have had the feeling of having to apply pressure on things to dissolve them. Whereas now, more and more, the pressure is imperceptible, it is immediate; as soon as the force to dissolve a whole set of things manifests, there is no resistance, everything dissolves; on the contrary, there is hardly any feeling of liberation — there is something which is amused again and says: "Oh, again! How many times one limits oneself...." How many times you think that you are advancing, continuously, smoothly, uninterruptedly, and yet how many times you set a little limit in front of yourself. It is not a big limit, for it is a very small thing in an immense whole, but it is a small limit to your action. And so when the Force acts to dissolve the limit, at first you feel liberated, you are glad; but now, it is not even that, it is a smile. Because it is not a feeling of liberation, it is simply like removing a stone from your path so that you can go on.

This idea of renunciation can only arise in a self-centred consciousness. Naturally, people — the ones I call altogether primitive — are attached to things: when they have something, they do not want to let it go! It seems so childish to me!... When they have to part with something, it hurts! Because they identify themselves with the things they have. But this is childishness. The true process behind all this is the amount of resistance in things that were formed on a certain basis of knowledge — which was a knowledge at a particular time and which is no longer so at another — a partial knowledge, not fleeting but impermanent. There is a whole set of things built upon this knowledge and they resist the force that says: "No! it is not true, (*laughing*) your basis is no longer true, let's take it away!" And then, oh! it hurts — this is what people experience as renunciation.[16]

THE MOTHER

The Secret behind Pain

> Pain and grief are Nature's reminder to the soul that the pleasure it enjoys is only a feeble hint of the real delight of existence. In each pain and torture of our being is the secret of a flame of rapture compared with which our greatest pleasures are only as dim flickerings. It is this secret which forms the attraction for the soul of the great ordeals, sufferings and fierce experiences of life which the nervous mind in us shuns and abhors.
>
> *Sri Aurobindo*

Quite naturally we ask ourselves what this secret is, towards which pain leads us. For a superficial and imperfect understanding, one could believe that it is pain which the soul is seeking. Nothing of the kind. The very nature of the soul is divine Delight, constant, unvarying, unconditioned, ecstatic; but it is true that if one can face suffering with courage, endurance, an unshakable faith in the divine Grace, if one can, instead of shunning suffering when it comes, enter into it with this will, this aspiration to go through it and find the luminous truth, the unvarying delight which is at the core of all things, the door of pain is often more direct, more immediate than that of satisfaction or contentment.

I am not speaking of pleasure because pleasure turns its back constantly and almost completely on this profound divine Delight.

Pleasure is a deceptive and perverse disguise which turns us away from our goal and we certainly should not seek it if we are eager to find the truth. Pleasure vaporises us; it deceives us, leads us astray. Pain brings us back to a deeper truth by obliging us to concentrate in order to be able to bear it, be able to face this thing that crushes us. It is in pain that one most easily finds the true strength again, when one is strong. It is in pain that one most easily finds the true faith again, the faith in something which is above and beyond all pain.

When one enjoys oneself and forgets, when one takes things as they come, tries to avoid being serious and looking life in the face, in a word when one seeks to forget, to forget that there is a problem to solve, that there is something to find, that we have a reason for existence and living, that we are not here just to pass our time and go away without having learnt or done anything, then one really wastes one's time, one misses the opportunity that has been given to us, this — I cannot say unique, but marvellous opportunity for an existence which is the field of progress, which is the moment in eternity when you can discover the secret of life; for this physical, material existence is a wonderful opportunity, a possibility given to you to find the purpose of life, to make you advance one step towards this deeper truth, to make you discover this secret which puts you into contact with the eternal rapture of the divine life.

(*Silence*)

I have already told you many a time that to seek suffering and pain is a morbid attitude which must be avoided, but to run away from them through forgetfulness, through a superficial, frivolous movement, through diversion, is cowardice. When pain comes, it comes to teach us something. The quicker we learn it, the more the need for pain diminishes, and when we know the secret, it will no longer be possible to suffer, for that secret reveals to us the reason, the cause, the origin of suffering, and the way to pass beyond it.

The secret is to emerge from the ego, get out of its prison, unite ourselves with the Divine, merge into Him, not to allow anything to separate us from Him. Then, once one has discovered this secret and realises it in one's being, pain loses its justification and suffering disappears. It is an all-powerful remedy, not only in the deeper parts of the being, in the soul, in the spiritual consciousness, but also in life and in the body.

There is no illness, no disorder which can resist the discovery of this secret and the putting of it into practice, not only in the higher parts of the being but in the cells of the body.

If one knows how to teach the cells the splendour that lies within them, if one knows how to make them understand the reality which makes them exist, gives them being, then they too enter the total harmony, and the physical disorder which causes the illness vanishes as do all other disorders of the being.

But for that one must be neither cowardly nor fearful.

When the physical disorder comes, one must not be afraid; one must not run away from it, must face it with courage, calmness, confidence, with the certitude that illness is a *falsehood* and that if one turns entirely, in full confidence, with a complete quietude to the divine Grace, It will settle in these cells as It is established in the depths of the being, and the cells themselves will share in the eternal Truth and Delight.[17]

THE MOTHER

Learning of Pure Delight

The meeting of man and God must always mean a penetration and entry of the Divine into the human and a self-immergence of man in the Divinity.

But that immergence is not in the nature of an annihilation. Extinction is not the fulfilment of all this search and passion, suffering and rapture. The game would never have been begun if that were to be its ending.

Delight is the secret. Learn of pure delight and thou shalt learn of God.

What then was the commencement of the whole matter? Existence that multiplied itself for sheer delight of being and plunged into numberless trillions of forms so that it might find itself innumerably.

Sri Aurobindo

How can one "learn of pure delight"?

First of all, to begin with, one must through an attentive

observation grow aware that desires and the satisfaction of desires give only a vague, uncertain pleasure, mixed, fugitive and altogether unsatisfactory. That is usually the starting-point.

Then, if one is a reasonable being, one must learn to discern what is desire and refrain from doing anything that may satisfy one's desires. One must reject them without trying to satisfy them. And so the first result is exactly one of the first observations stated by the Buddha in his teaching: there is an infinitely greater delight in conquering and eliminating a desire than in satisfying it. Every sincere and steadfast seeker will realise after some time, sooner or later, at times very soon, that this is an absolute truth, and that the delight felt in overcoming a desire is incomparably higher than the small pleasure, so fleeting and mixed, which may be found in the satisfaction of his desires. That is the second step.

Naturally, with this continuous discipline, in a very short time the desires will keep their distance and will no longer bother you. So you will be free to enter a little more deeply into your being and open yourself in an aspiration to... the Giver of Delight, the divine Element, the divine Grace. And if this is done with a sincere self-giving — something that gives itself, offers itself and expects nothing in exchange for its offering — one will feel that kind of sweet warmth, comfortable, intimate, radiant, which fills the heart and is the herald of Delight.

After this, the path is easy.[18]

THE MOTHER

Delight of Being

There comes a time when one begins to be almost ready, when one can feel in everything, every object, in every movement, in every vibration, in all the things around — not only people and conscious beings, but things, objects; not only trees and plants and living things, but simply any object one uses, the things around one — this delight, this delight of being, of being just as one is, simply being. And one sees that all this vibrates like that. One touches a thing and feels this delight. But naturally, I say, one must have followed the discipline I spoke about at the beginning; otherwise, so long as one has a desire, a preference, an attachment or affinities and repulsions and all that, one cannot — one cannot.

And so long as one finds pleasures — pleasure, well, yes, vital or physical pleasure in a thing — one cannot feel this delight. For this delight is everywhere. This delight is something very subtle. One moves in the midst of things and it is as though they were all singing to you their delight. There comes a time when it becomes very familiar in the life around you. Of course, I must admit that it is a little more difficult to feel it in human beings, because there are all their mental and vital formations which come into the field of perception and disturb it. There is too much of this kind of egoistic asperity which gets mixed with things, so it is more difficult to contact the Delight there. But even in animals one feels it; it is already a little more difficult than in plants. But in plants, in flowers, it is so wonderful! They speak all their joy, they express it. And as I said, in all familiar objects, the things around you, which you use, there is a state of consciousness in which each one is happy to be, just as it is. So at that moment one knows one has touched true Delight. And it is not conditioned. I mean it does not depend upon... it depends on nothing. It does not depend on outer circumstances, does not depend on a more or less favourable state, it does not depend on anything: it is a communion with the *raison d'être* of the universe.

And when this comes it fills all the cells of the body. It is not even a thing which is thought out — one does not reason, does not analyse, it is not that: it is a *state* in which one lives. And when the body shares in it, it is so fresh — so fresh, so spontaneous, so... it no longer turns back upon itself, there is no longer any sense of self-observation, of self-analysis or of analysing things. All that is like a canticle of joyous vibrations, but very, very quiet, without violence, without passion, nothing of all that. It is very subtle and very intense at the same time, and when it comes, it seems that the whole universe is a marvellous harmony. Even what is to the ordinary human consciousness ugly, unpleasant, appears marvellous.

Unfortunately, as I said, people, circumstances, all that, with all those mental and vital formations — that disturbs it all the time. Then one is obliged to return to this ignorant, blind perception of things. But otherwise, as soon as all this stops and one can get out of it... everything changes. As he says there, at the end: everything changes. A marvellous harmony. And it is all Delight, true Delight, real Delight.

This demands a little work.

And this discipline I spoke about, which one must undergo, if it is practised with the aim of finding Delight, the result is delayed, for an egoistic element is introduced into it, it is done with an aim and is no longer an offering, it is a demand, and then.... It comes, it will come, even if it takes much longer — when one asks nothing, expects nothing, hopes for nothing, when it is simply that, it is self-giving and aspiration, and the spontaneous need without any bargaining — the need to be divine, that's all.[19]

THE MOTHER

5. SIN, EVIL AND UGLINESS

Judging

Unless your vision is *constantly* the vision of the Divine in all things, you have not only no right but no capacity to judge the state which others are in. And to pronounce a judgment on someone without having this vision spontaneously, effortlessly, is precisely an example of the mental presumptuousness of which Sri Aurobindo always spoke.... And it so happens that one who has the vision, the consciousness, who is capable of seeing the truth in all things, never feels the need to judge anything whatever. For he understands everything and knows everything. Therefore, once and for all, you must tell yourselves that the moment you begin to judge things, people, circumstances, you are in the most total human ignorance.

In short, one could put it like this: when one understands, one no longer judges and when one judges, it means that one doesn't know.

Judging people is one of the first things which must be totally swept away from the consciousness before you can take even a step on the supramental path, because that is not a material progress or a bodily progress, it is only a very little progress of thought, mental progress. And unless you have swept your mind clean of all its ignorance, you cannot hope to take a step on the supramental path.

In fact, you have said something terrible. When you said, "I cannot speak to his soul if he is a brute", well, you have given yourself away... you have stuck a label on yourself. There you are.

All those who have truly and sincerely had the experience of the divine Presence, all those who have truly been in contact with the Divine, have always said the same thing: that sometimes, even often, it is in what is most decried by men, most despised by men, most condemned by human "wisdom", that one can see the divine light shining.

They are not mere words, they are living experiences.

All these ideas of good and evil, good and bad, higher, lower, all these notions belong to the ignorance of the human mind, and if one really wants to come into contact with the divine life, one must liberate oneself totally from this ignorance, one must rise to a region of consciousness where these things have *no* reality. The feeling of superiority and inferiority completely disappears, it is replaced by something else which is of a very different nature — a sort of capacity for filtering appearances, penetrating behind masks, shifting the point of view.

And these are not words, it is altogether true that *everything* changes its appearance, totally, that life and things are completely different from what they appear to be.[20]

THE MOTHER

Attitude Towards Sin

To hate the sinner is the worst sin, for it is hating God; yet he who commits it glories in his superior virtue.

Sri Aurobindo

When we enter into a certain state of consciousness, we see clearly that we are capable of anything and that in fact there is not a single "sin" that is not potentially our sin. Is this impression correct? And yet we revolt against and feel an aversion for certain things: there is always something somewhere which we cannot accept. Why? What is the true attitude, the effective attitude in face of evil?

There is not a single sin that is not our sin.... You have this experience when for some reason or other — depending on the case — you come into contact with the universal state of consciousness — not in its limitless essence, but on any level of Matter. There is an atomic consciousness; there is a purely material consciousness; and there is, even more, a general psychological consciousness. When by going within, by a kind of withdrawal from the ego, you come into contact with this zone of consciousness, let us say, a terrestrial or collective human psychological zone — there is a difference, "collective human" is restrictive, whereas "terrestrial" includes many animal movements, even plant movements; but as in the present case the moral notion of guilt, sin, evil belongs exclusively to the human consciousness, we will say simply the collective human psychological consciousness — when you come into contact with that through this identification, naturally you feel or see or know that you are capable of any human movement anywhere. It is to some extent a truth-consciousness — this egoistic sense of what belongs and does not belong to you, of what you can do and cannot do, disappears at that time; you become aware that the fundamental structure of the human consciousness is such that any human being is capable of doing anything at all. And since you are in a truth-consciousness, at the same time you have the feeling that judgments or aversions, or rejection, are absurd. *Everything* is potentially there. And if certain currents of force — which you usually cannot trace; you see them come and go, but as a rule their origin and direction are unknown — if any one of these currents enters into you, it can make you do anything.

If you could always remain in this state of consciousness, after some time — provided you maintained within you the flame of Agni, the flame of purification and progress — you would be able not only to prevent these movements from taking an active form in you and expressing themselves materially, but also to act on the very nature of the movement and transform it. But, of course, unless you have attained a very high degree of realisation, it will be practically impossible to maintain this state of consciousness for long. Almost immediately you fall back into the egoistic consciousness of the separate self. And then all the difficulties come back: the disgust, the revolt against certain things, the horror they arouse in you, etc.

It is probable — it is even certain — that until you are yourself completely transformed, these movements of disgust and revolt are needed so that you can do *in yourself* what has to be done to shut the door. For after all, the problem is not to allow them to manifest themselves.

In another aphorism Sri Aurobindo says — I no longer remember his exact words — that sin is merely something which is not in its right place. In this perpetual Becoming nothing ever repeats itself, and there are things that disappear, so to speak, into the past; and when their disappearance becomes necessary these things become, for our very limited consciousness, bad and repulsive. And we revolt against them because their time is over. But if we had the overall view, if we could contain within ourselves the past, the present and the future all at once — as it is somewhere above — we would see the relativity of these things and that it is above all the progressive Force of evolution that gives us the will to reject; and that wherever they are in their right place, they are quite acceptable. Only, it is practically impossible to have this experience unless you have the total vision, that is to say, the vision that belongs to the Supreme alone! Therefore you must first of all identify yourself with the Supreme; then, afterwards, with this identification, you can return to a sufficiently exteriorised consciousness and see things as they are. But that is the principle, and to the extent that you are capable of realising it, you reach a state of consciousness where you can look at everything with a smile of total certitude that everything is as it should be.

Naturally, people who do not think deeply enough will say, "Ah, but if we saw that everything is as it should be, nothing would move!" No, you cannot prevent things from moving! Even for a fraction of a second they do not stop moving. It is a continuous, total transformation, a movement that never ceases. And because it is difficult for us to feel like this, it is possible for us to imagine that if we were to enter into certain states of consciousness, things would not change. But even if we were to enter into an apparently total inertia, things would continue to change and so would we!

Basically, disgust, revolt, anger, all these movements of violence are necessarily movements of ignorance and limitation, with all the weakness that limitation represents. Revolt is a weakness — it is the feeling of an impotent will.

You will — or you think you will — you feel, you see that things are not as they should be and you revolt against whatever does not agree with what you see. But if you were all-powerful, if your will and your vision were all-powerful, there would be no occasion for you to revolt, you would always see that all things are as they should be. If we go to the highest level and unite with the consciousness of the supreme Will, we see, at every second, at every moment of the universe, that all is exactly as it should be, exactly as the Supreme wills it. That is omnipotence. And all movements of violence become not only unnecessary but utterly ridiculous.

Therefore there is only one solution: to unite ourselves by aspiration, concentration, interiorisation and identification with the supreme Will. And that is both omnipotence and perfect freedom at the same time. And that is the only omnipotence and the only freedom; everything else is an approximation. You may be on the way, but it is not the entire thing. So if you experience this, you realise that with this supreme freedom and supreme power there is also a total peace and a serenity that never fails. Therefore, if you feel something which is not that, a revolt, a disgust, something which you cannot accept, it means that *in you* there is a part which has not been touched by the transformation, something which has kept the old consciousness, something which is still on the path — that is all.[21]

THE MOTHER

Sharing the Burden of Sin

> Examine thyself without pity, then thou wilt be more charitable and pitiful to others. —*Sri Aurobindo*

Very good!

It is very good, very good for everybody, particularly for people who think themselves very superior.

But this really corresponds to something very profound.

In fact, this is an experience which I have been having for some time. It is almost like a reversal of attitude.

Indeed, men have always considered themselves victims harassed by adverse forces; those who are courageous fight, the others complain. But I have an increasingly concrete vision of the role that the adverse forces play in the creation, of the almost absolute necessity for them, so that there can be progress and for the creation to become its Origin once again — and such a clear vision that instead of asking for the conversion or abolition of the adverse forces one must realise one's own transformation, pray for it and carry it out. This is from the terrestrial point of view, I am not taking the individual standpoint. We know the individual standpoint; this is from the terrestrial point of view. It was the sudden vision of all the error, all the misunderstanding, all the ignorance and obscurity, and even worse, all the bad will in the terrestrial consciousness which felt responsible for the perpetuation of these adverse beings and forces and which offered them in a great aspiration — more than an aspiration, a kind of holocaust — so that the adverse forces might disappear and have no further reason to exist, so that they might no longer be there to point out everything that has to be changed.

Their presence was made unavoidable by all these things that were negations of the divine life. And this movement of offering of the earth consciousness to the Supreme, in an extraordinary intensity, was like a redemption so that the adverse forces might disappear.

It was a very intense experience which expressed itself like this: "Take all the faults I have committed, take them all, accept them, efface them so that these forces may disappear."

This aphorism is the same thing from the other end, it is the same thing in essence. As long as it is possible for a human consciousness to feel, act, think or be contrary to the great divine Becoming, it is impossible to blame anyone else for it; it is impossible to blame the adverse forces which are maintained in creation as the means of making you see and feel all the progress that has yet to be made.

(*Silence*)

The state I found myself in was like a memory — a memory that is eternally present — of that Consciousness of supreme Love which the Lord emanated upon earth, in the earth — *in* the earth — to bring it back to Him. For that was truly a descent into the most total negation of the Divine, the negation of the very essence of the divine Nature, and therefore a renunciation of the divine state in order to accept earth's obscurity and bring earth back to the divine state. And unless this supreme Love becomes all-powerfully conscious here on earth, the return can never be final.

This experience came after the vision of the great divine Becoming, and I asked myself, "Since this world is progressive, since it is becoming more and more the Divine, will there not always be this intensely painful feeling of the thing which is undivine, of the state which is undivine compared to the one which is to come? Will there not always be what we call 'adverse forces', that is, something which is not following the movement harmoniously?" Then the answer came, the vision came: no, indeed the time for this possibility is near, the time for the manifestation of that essence of perfect Love which can transform this unconsciousness, this ignorance and the bad will which results from it into a progression that is luminous, joyful, eager for perfection and all-inclusive.

It was very concrete.

And this corresponds to a state in which one is so *perfectly* identified with all that is, that one becomes all that is anti-divine in a concrete way, and that one can offer it — one can offer it and truly transform it by offering it.

Basically, this kind of will for purity, for good, in men — which expresses itself in the ordinary mentality as the need to be virtuous — is the *great obstacle* to true self-giving. This is the origin of Falsehood and even more the very source of hypocrisy — the refusal to accept to take upon oneself one's own share of the burden of difficulties. And in this aphorism Sri Aurobindo has gone straight to this point in a very simple way.

Do not try to appear virtuous. See how much you are united, one with everything that is anti-divine. Take your share of the burden, accept yourselves to be impure and false and in that way you will be able to take up the Shadow and offer it. And in so far as you are capable of taking it and offering it, then things will change.

Do not try to be among the pure. Accept to be with those who are in darkness and give it all with total love.[22]

THE MOTHER

Helping to Cure Evil and Ugliness

> To feel and love the God of beauty and good in the ugly and the evil, and still yearn in utter love to heal it of its ugliness and its evil, this is real virtue and morality.
>
> *Sri Aurobindo*

> *How can one help to cure the evil and the ugliness that one sees everywhere? Through love? What is the power of love? How can an individual phenomenon of consciousness act on the rest of mankind?*

How can one help to cure evil and ugliness?... One may say that there is a kind of hierarchy of collaboration or action: there is a negative help and a positive help.

To begin with, there is a way that might be called negative, the way provided by Buddhism and kindred religions: not to see. First of all, to be in such a state of purity and beauty that you do not perceive ugliness and evil — it is like something that does not touch you because it does not exist in you.

That is the perfection of the negative method. It is quite elementary: never to notice evil, never to speak of the evil in others, not to perpetuate these vibrations by observation, by criticism, by insistence on what is bad. That is what the

Buddha taught: each time you speak of an evil, you help to spread it.

This barely touches the problem.

Yet it should be a very general rule. But people who criticise have an answer for that; they say, "If you do not see the evil, you will never be able to cure it. If you leave someone in his ugliness, he will never get out of it." This is not true, but that is how they justify their behaviour. So in this aphorism Sri Aurobindo forestalls these objections: it is not because of ignorance or unconsciousness or indifference that you do not see the evil — you are quite capable of seeing it, even of feeling it, but you refuse to help to spread it by giving it the force of your attention and the support of your consciousness. And for that you must yourself be above this perception and feeling; you must be able to see the evil or the ugliness without suffering from it, without being shocked or disturbed by it. You see it from a height where these things do not exist, but you have the conscious perception of it, you are not affected by it, you are free. This is the first step.

The second step is to be *positively* conscious of the supreme Good and supreme Beauty behind all things, which sustains all things and enables them to exist. When you see Him, you are able to perceive Him behind this mask and this distortion; even this ugliness, this wickedness, this evil is a disguise of Something which is essentially beautiful or good, luminous, pure.

Then comes the *true* collaboration, for when you have this vision, this perception, when you live in this consciousness, it also gives you the power to *draw* That down into the manifestation, to the earth, and to bring It into contact with what now distorts and disguises, so that little by little this distortion and this disguise are transformed by the influence of the Truth that is behind.

Here we are at the very summit of the scale of collaboration.

In this way it is not necessary to introduce the principle of love into the explanation. But if you want to know or understand the nature of the Force or the Power that enables or brings about this transformation—particularly where evil is concerned, but also with ugliness to a certain extent—you see that love is obviously the most potent and integral of all powers—integral in the sense that it applies in all cases. It is even more powerful than the power of purification which dissolves all bad will and which is, as it were, the master of the adverse forces, but which has not the direct power of transformation. The power of purification first dissolves in order to allow the transformation afterwards. It destroys one form in order to be able to create a better one, whereas love need not dissolve in order to transform; it possesses the direct power of transformation. Love is like a flame that changes what is hard into something malleable and even sublimates this malleable thing into a kind of purified vapour—it does not destroy, it transforms.

In its essence, in its origin, love is like a flame, a white flame which overcomes *all* resistances. You can experience this yourself: whatever the difficulty in your being, whatever the burden of accumulated error, ignorance, incapacity and bad will, a single *second* of this pure, essential, supreme love dissolves it as in an all-powerful flame; a single moment and a whole past can disappear; a single instant in which you *touch* it in its essence and a whole burden is consumed.

And it is very easy to explain how a person who has this experience can spread it, can act on others; because to have the experience you must touch the one, supreme Essence of the whole manifestation, the Origin and the Essence, the Source and the Reality of all that is; and at once you enter the realm of Unity — there is no longer any separation of individuals, there is only one single vibration that can be repeated indefinitely in external form.*

If you rise high enough, you find yourself at the heart of all things. And what is manifest in this heart can manifest in all things. That is the great secret, the secret of the divine incarnation in an individual form, because in the normal course of things what manifests at the centre is realised in the external form only with the awakening and the response of the will in the individual form. Whereas if the central Will is represented constantly and permanently in an individual being, this individual being can serve as an intermediary between this Will and all beings, and will for them. Everything this individual being perceives and offers in his consciousness to the supreme Will is answered as if it came from each individual being. And if for any reason the individual elements have a more or less conscious and voluntary relation with that representative being, their relation increases the efficacy, the effectiveness of the representative

* Later the disciple asked Mother: "Is it one single vibration which *can be repeated* indefinitely or which *is repeated* indefinitely?" Mother answered: "I meant several things at the same time. This single vibration is static everywhere, but when one realises it consciously, one has the power of making it active wherever one directs it; that is to say, one doesn't move anything, but the stress of the consciousness makes it active wherever one directs one's consciousness."

individual; and thus the supreme Action can act in Matter in a much more concrete and permanent manner. That is the reason for these descents of consciousness — which we may describe as "polarised", for they always come to earth with a definite purpose and for a special realisation, with a mission — a mission which is decided upon, determined before the incarnation. These are the great stages of the supreme incarnations on earth.

And when the day comes for the manifestation of supreme love, for the crystallised, concentrated descent of supreme love, that will truly be the hour of transformation. For nothing will be able to resist That.

But since it is all-powerful, some receptivity must be prepared on earth so that the effects are not shattering. Sri Aurobindo has explained this in one of his letters. Someone asked him, "Why does it not come immediately?" He answered something like this: if divine love were to manifest in its essence upon earth, it would be like a bombshell; because the earth is neither supple nor receptive enough to be able to widen itself to the dimensions of this love. It not only needs to open, but to widen itself and to become more supple — Matter is still too rigid. And even the substance of the physical consciousness — not only the most material Matter, but the substance of the physical consciousness — is too rigid.[23]

THE MOTHER

6. LIGHT ON THE PATH

Preparing the Path

... Have you never had the feeling in your life that you were on the way towards something? No? One doesn't have the impression that when he is born he begins to set his feet on a road which is going to lead him by a curve through his whole life? That's the image. So if you take the path which must lead you to a spiritual realisation, well, it means that all your actions are deliberately going to be directed to this goal. And so he [Sri Aurobindo] says that there is a bit of the way which is under the control of reason and that reason, if you follow it, helps you to go forward here without your making mistakes too often. For it is quite remarkable that in life you start without knowing anything, and that at each step you take you have to learn, and that usually you come to the end, to the end of the path, without having learnt anything very much, because too often you make mistakes and you have nothing to guide you.

Ordinary people enter life without even knowing what it is to live, and at each step they have to learn how to live. And before knowing what they want to realise, they must at least know how to walk; as we teach a tiny little child how to walk, in life one has also to learn how to live. Which people know how to live? And it is through experience, through mistakes, through all kinds of misfortunes and troubles of every sort that gradually one begins to be what is called reasonable, that is, when one has made a mistake a certain number of times and has had troublesome consequences from this mistake, one learns not to make it again. But there is a moment, when the brain is developed enough and you can use the reason, well, reason can help you to reduce the number of these mistakes, to teach you to walk the path without stumbling too often.

The immense majority of human beings are born, live and die without knowing why this has happened to them. They take it... it is like that; they are born, they live, they have what they call their joys and their sorrows, and they come to the end and go away. They came in and went out without learning anything. This indeed is the immense majority.

There is among them a small number of people called the *élite*, who try to know what has happened to them, why they are upon earth and why all that happens to them happens. Then among these there are some who use their reason and they find a way of walking properly on the path, much faster than the others. These are reasonable beings.

Now there is a handful—a big handful—of people who are born with the feeling that there is something else to find in life, a higher purpose to life, that there is an aim, and they strive to find it. So for these the path goes beyond reason, to regions which they have to explore either with or without help, as chance takes them, and they must then discover the higher worlds. But there are not many of this kind. I don't know how many of these there are now in the world, but I have the impression that they could still be counted. So for these it depends on when they begin.

Now there are beings, I think, who are born and whose rational period of life may begin very early, when they are very young, and it may last for a very short time; and then they are almost immediately ready to set out on new and unexplored paths towards the higher realities. But in order to set out on these paths without fear and without any danger, one must have organised his being with the help of reason around the highest centre he consciously possesses, and organised it in such a way that it is inwardly in his control and he has not to say at every moment, "Ah! I have done this, I don't know why. Ah! That's happened to me, I don't know why" — and always it is "I don't know, I don't know, I don't know", and as long as it is like that, the path is somewhat dangerous. Only when one does what he wants, knows what he wants, does what he wants and is able to direct himself with certitude, without being tossed about by the hazards of life, then one can go forward on the suprarational paths fearlessly, unhesitatingly and with the least danger. But one need not be very old for this to happen. One can begin very young; even a child of five can already make use of reason to control himself; I know it. There is enough mental organisation in the being in these little tots* who look so spontaneous and irresponsible; there is enough cerebral organisation for them to organise themselves, their life, their nature, their movements, actions and thoughts with reason.[24]

THE MOTHER

The Call and the Consecration

All Yoga is in its nature a new birth; it is a birth out of the

* The Mother is apparently referring to the little children studying in the Sri Aurobindo Ashram school. — Ed.

ordinary, the mentalised material life of man into a higher spiritual consciousness and a greater and diviner being. No Yoga can be successfully undertaken and followed unless there is a strong awakening to the necessity of that larger spiritual existence. The soul that is called to this deep and vast inward change, may arrive in different ways to the initial departure. It may come to it by its own natural development which has been leading it unconsciously towards the awakening; it may reach it through the influence of a religion or the attraction of a philosophy; it may approach it by a slow illumination or leap to it by a sudden touch or shock; it may be pushed or led to it by the pressure of outward circumstances or by an inward necessity, by a single word that breaks the seals of the mind or by long reflection, by the distant example of one who has trod the path or by contact and daily influence. According to the nature and the circumstances the call will come.

But in whatever way it comes, there must be a decision of the mind and the will and, as its result, a complete and effective self-consecration. The acceptance of a new spiritual idea-force and upward orientation in the being, an illumination, a turning or conversion seized on by the will and the heart's aspiration, — this is the momentous act which contains as in a seed all the results that the Yoga has to give. The mere idea or intellectual seeking of something higher beyond, however strongly grasped by the mind's interest, is ineffective unless it is seized on by the heart as the one thing desirable and by the will as the one thing to be done. For truth of the Spirit has not to be merely thought but to be lived, and to live it demands a unified single-mindedness of the being; so great a change as is contemplated by the

Yoga is not to be effected by a divided will or by a small portion of the energy or by a hesitating mind. He who seeks the Divine must consecrate himself to God and to God only.

If the change comes suddenly and decisively by an overpowering influence, there is no further essential or lasting difficulty. The choice follows upon the thought, or is simultaneous with it, and the self-consecration follows upon the choice. The feet are already set upon the path, even if they seem at first to wander uncertainly and even though the path itself may be only obscurely seen and the knowledge of the goal may be imperfect. The secret Teacher, the inner Guide is already at work, though he may not yet manifest himself or may not yet appear in the person of his human representative. Whatever difficulties and hesitations may ensue, they cannot eventually prevail against the power of the experience that has turned the current of the life. The call, once decisive, stands; the thing that has been born cannot eventually be stifled. Even if the force of circumstances prevents a regular pursuit or a full practical self-consecration from the first, still the mind has taken its bent and persists and returns with an ever-increasing effect upon its leading preoccupation. There is an ineluctable persistence of the inner being, and against it circumstances are in the end powerless, and no weakness in the nature can for long be an obstacle.

But this is not always the manner of the commencement. The sadhaka is often led gradually and there is a long space between the first turning of the mind and the full assent of the nature to the thing towards which it turns. There may at first be only a vivid intellectual interest, a forcible attraction towards the idea and some imperfect form of practice. Or perhaps there is an effort not favoured by the whole nature, a decision or a turn imposed by an intellectual influence or dictated by personal affection and admiration for someone who is himself consecrated and devoted to the Highest. In such cases, a long period of preparation may be necessary before there comes the irrevocable consecration; and in some instances it may not come. There may be some advance, there may be a strong effort, even much purification and many experiences other than those that are central or supreme; but the life will either be spent in preparation or, a certain stage having been reached, the mind pushed by an insufficient driving-force may rest content at the limit of the effort possible to it. Or there may even be a recoil to the lower life, — what is called in the ordinary parlance of Yoga a fall from the path. This lapse happens because there is a defect at the very centre. The intellect has been interested, the heart attracted, the will has strung itself to the effort, but the whole nature has not been taken captive by the Divine. It has only acquiesced in the interest, the attraction or the endeavour. There has been an experiment, perhaps even an eager experiment, but not a total self-giving to an imperative need of the soul or to an unforsakable ideal. Even such imperfect Yoga has not been wasted; for no upward effort is made in vain. Even if it fails in the present or arrives only at some preparatory stage or preliminary realisation, it has yet determined the soul's future.

But if we desire to make the most of the opportunity that this life gives us, if we wish to respond adequately to the call we have received and to attain to the goal we have glimpsed, not merely advance a little towards it, it is essential that there should be an entire self-giving. The secret of success in Yoga is to regard it not as one of the aims to be pursued in life, but as the one and only aim, not as an important part of life, but as the whole of life.[25]

SRI AUROBINDO

Zeal for the Lord

The development of the experience in its rapidity, its amplitude, the intensity and power of its results, depends primarily, in the beginning of the path and long after, on the aspiration and personal effort of the sadhaka. The process of Yoga is a turning of the human soul from the egoistic state of consciousness absorbed in the outward appearances and attractions of things to a higher state in which the Transcendent and Universal can pour itself into the individual mould and transform it. The first determining element of the siddhi is, therefore, the intensity of the turning, the force which directs the soul inward. The power of aspiration of the heart, the force of the will, the concentration of the mind, the perseverance and determination of the applied energy are the measure of that intensity. The ideal sadhaka should be able to say in the Biblical phrase, "My zeal for the Lord has eaten me up." It is this zeal for the Lord, — *utsāha*, the zeal of the whole nature for its divine results, *vyākulatā*, the heart's eagerness for the attainment of the Divine, — that devours the ego and breaks up the limitations of its petty and narrow mould for the full and wide reception of that which it seeks, that which, being universal, exceeds and, being transcendent, surpasses even the largest and highest individual self and nature.

But this is only one side of the force that works for perfection. The process of the integral Yoga has three stages, not indeed sharply distinguished or separate, but in a certain measure successive. There must be, first, the effort towards at least an initial and enabling self-transcendence and contact with the Divine; next, the reception of that which transcends, that with which we have gained communion, into ourselves for the transformation of our whole conscious being; last, the utilisation of our transformed humanity as a divine centre in the world. So long as the contact with the Divine is not in some considerable degree established, so long as there is not some measure of sustained identity, *sȳujya*, the element of personal effort must normally predominate. But in proportion as this contact establishes itself, the sadhaka must become conscious that a force other than his own, a force transcending his egoistic endeavour and capacity, is at work in him and to this Power he learns progressively to submit himself and delivers up to it the charge of his Yoga. In the end his own will and force become one with the higher Power; he merges them in the divine Will and its transcendent and universal Force. He finds it thenceforward presiding over the necessary transformation of his mental, vital and physical being with an impartial wisdom and provident effectivity of which the eager and interested ego is not capable. It is when this identification and this self-merging are complete that the divine centre in the world is ready. Purified, liberated, plastic, illumined, it can begin to serve as a means for the direct action of a supreme Power in the larger Yoga of humanity or superhumanity, of the earth's spiritual progression or its transformation.[3]

SRI AUROBINDO

When Prayer and Meditation Become Mechanical

It is from someone who is trying to prepare himself to receive the Supermind, and in this preparation, among other things come prayer and meditation. And then there is this reflection which is very frank and which very few would have the courage to make. Here it is:

> *"I begin to meditate and pray ardently and fervently, my aspiration is intense and my prayer full of devotion; and then, after a certain length of time — sometimes short, sometimes long — the aspiration becomes mechanical and the prayer purely verbal. What should I do?"*

This is not an individual case, it is extremely common. I have already said this a number of times, but still it was in passing — that people who claim to meditate for hours every day and spend their whole day praying, to me it seems that three-fourths of the time it must be absolutely mechanical; that is to say, it loses all its sincerity. For human nature is not made for that and the human mind is not built that way.

In order to concentrate and meditate one must do an exercise which I could call the "mental muscle-building" of concentration. One must really make an effort — as one makes a muscular effort, for instance, to lift a weight — if you want the concentration to be sincere and not artificial.

The same thing for the urge of prayer: suddenly a flame is lit, you feel an enthusiastic *élan*, a great fervour, and express it in words which, to be true, must be spontaneous. This must come from the heart, directly, with ardour, without passing through the head. That is a prayer. If there are just words jostling in your head, it is no longer a prayer. Well, if you don't throw more fuel into the flame, after a time it dies out. If you do not give your muscles time to relax, if you don't slacken the movement, your muscles lose the capacity of taking strains. So it is quite natural, and even indispensable, for the intensity of the movement to cease after a certain time. Naturally, someone who is accustomed to lifting weights can do it much longer than one who has never done it before. It is the same thing; someone who is accustomed to concentration can concentrate much longer than one who is not in the habit. But for everybody there comes a time when one must let go, relax, in order to begin again. Therefore, whether immediately or after a few minutes or a few hours, if the movement becomes mechanical, it means that you have relaxed and that you need no longer pretend that you are meditating. It is better to do something useful.

If you cannot manage to do a little exercise, for instance, in order to neutralise the effect of the mental tension, you may read or try to note down what happened to you, you may express things. Then that produces a relaxation, the necessary relaxation. But the duration of the meditation is only relatively important; its length simply shows how far you are accustomed to this activity.

Of course, this may increase a great deal, but there is always a limit; and when the limit is reached one must stop, that's all. It is not an insincerity, it is an incapacity. What becomes insincere is if you pretend to meditate when you are no longer meditating or you say prayers like many people who go to the temple or to church, perform ceremonies and repeat their prayers as one repeats a more or less well-learnt lesson. Then it is no longer either prayer or meditation, it is simply a profession. It is not interesting.[27]

THE MOTHER

Keeping the Intensity of the Inner Consciousness

Oh, this should not be very difficult. Truly it should not be very difficult. For me what seems difficult is not to keep a kind of intensity of inner consciousness, to be separated from it; this seems something impossible. Once one catches that within oneself, how can one separate oneself from it, if you have had it once, if it has become a reality for you, this consciousness and this inner union with the psychic, and this consciousness and intensity of aspiration, and this flame which is always lit? Why, whatever one may be doing, this cannot be extinguished, it is always there.

It seems to me that to separate oneself from it, once it is there, you must close a door, you must deliberately close the door, like this, upon it, and say, "I am no longer interested in it." But if one truly has the will to keep the contact, it doesn't seem very difficult to me. It seems to me that one must really have the will to turn one's back upon it for it to go away; otherwise it is there, behind everything, all things, constantly. And if on the contrary one has made it a habit, when saying something, when making a movement, simply a movement or doing anything at all, to refer always to that, in there, not to feel capable of doing something without having that at the back, there, to tell you, "Yes, this way, not that way. That, no, not that, this", then it is difficult to live without it.

Some people, because it troubles them, because it puts a control on their impulses and they want to feel absolutely free and independent (what they call independent), seem deliberately to bang the door, like that, they slam the door violently to stop it. Then naturally, once it is done, it is done; then one becomes something so superficial, so weak, so petty, so ignorant, so stupid! How can one bear to be like that? It seems to me that immediately the instinct would be to take a step backwards, open the door hurriedly and put oneself again into contact, saying, "No, no, no, not this state, not this frightful state of ignorance" — in which you don't even know what you ought to say or ought not to say, what you ought to do or ought not to do, where you should go or should not go, nothing, nothing, you are in an obscure and incoherent immensity. It is a dreadful state. But when the door is open and this thing is behind, it is absolutely comfortable at every minute, as though one were leaning one's back against a great light, a great consciousness, like this... "Ah, now, here we are, this is what ought to be done, that's what ought to be said, this is the movement to be made", etc. So, then one is comfortable, quiet, without anguish, without any problem, without any anxiety. One does what one wants to do; whether people take it more or less well is their affair, but for oneself it is like that.[28]

THE MOTHER

Awakening One's Yogashakti

How can one awaken his Yogashakti?

It depends on this: when one thinks that it is the most important thing in his life. That's all.

Some people sit in meditation, concentrate on the base of the vertebral column and want it very much to awake, but that's not enough. It is when truly it becomes the most important thing in one's life, when all the rest seems to have lost all taste, all interest, all importance, when one feels within that one is born for this, that one is here upon earth for this, and that it is the only thing that truly counts, then that's enough.

One can concentrate on the different centres; but sometimes one concentrates for so long, with so much effort, and has no result. And then one day something shakes you, you feel that you are going to lose your footing, you have to cling on to something; then you cling within yourself to the idea of union with the Divine, the idea of the divine Presence, the idea of the transformation of the consciousness, and you aspire, you want, you try to organise your feelings, movements, impulses around this. And it comes.

Some people have recommended all kinds of methods; probably these were methods which had succeeded in their case; but to tell the truth, one must find one's own method, it is only after having done the thing that one knows how it should be done, not before.

If one knows it beforehand, one makes a mental construction and risks greatly living in his mental construction, which is an illusion; because when the mind builds certain conditions and then they are realised, there are many chances of there being mostly pure mental construction which is not the experience itself but its image. So for all these truly spiritual experiences I think it is wiser to have them before knowing them. If one knows them, one imitates them, one doesn't have them, one imagines oneself having them; whereas if one knows nothing — how things are and how they ought to happen, what should happen and how it will come about — if one knows nothing about all this, then by keeping very still and making a kind of inner sorting out within one's being, one can suddenly have the experience, and then later knows what one has had. It is over, and one knows how it has to be done when one has done it — afterwards. Like that it is sure.

One may obviously make use of his imagination, imagine the Kundalini and try to pull it upwards. But one can also tell himself tales like this. I have had so many instances of people who described their experiences to me exactly as they are described in books, knowing all the words and putting down all the details, and then I asked them just a little question like that, casually: that if they had had the experience they should have known or felt a certain thing, and as this was not in the books, they could not answer.

Sweet Mother, what is the significance of the thousand-petalled lotus?

That is how they describe it. It is because there's a centre there, very, very complicated. I think it means the countless powers of thought, it is the multiplicity of knowledge in all its forms. It must be that. Why, this is still another instance:

people who have read, studied, and have the experience afterwards, well, they always describe it like that, with names they have picked up in books and with descriptions of the lotuses as they are given in books; but those who have the spontaneous experience without having read or learnt anything before having it, they describe it altogether vividly, with an individual reality, so to say. Each one approaches the experience in his own way. When these centres awake... it is a fact that there are centres, and it's a fact that they awake, and it's a fact that this changes vastly the whole working of the consciousness and energy, but the description, if it is spontaneous and sincere, is different for everyone. One can have the feeling of a similarity with something, but giving a fixed and precise description of what happens is always an intervention of the mind.

This phenomenon is very real, concrete, it is felt with all the reality and intensity of even a physical phenomenon. But each person describes it with a form particular to himself, except as I say, when he has read and studied, and his brain is full of all that is written in books; then automatically what he has read gives a form to his experience, and this takes away from it something of the spontaneity which gives such an impression of being sincere and truthful; it becomes a mental construction. If you have read and read much that it is like a serpent which is coiled up, well, quite naturally when you concentrate and try to awaken it, you see a serpent which is coiled, because you think about it like that. If you are told about a thousand-petalled lotus, you see a thousand-petalled lotus. But it is a mental superimposition upon the fact of the experience itself. But the feeling of something that's innumerable, that's one and innumerable at the same time, and that kind of impression of something opening, awakening, beginning to vibrate, responding to the forces and giving you an intensity of light, of understanding, of opening to higher regions, this is... the substance of the experience. Yet when you begin to describe it with images which you have found in books, it is as though suddenly you were making it either superficial — fossilised, so to say — or artificial or even insincere.

Always the most interesting cases for me have been those of people who had read nothing but had a very ardent aspiration and came to me saying, "Something funny has happened to me, I had this extraordinary experience, what can it mean truly?" And then they describe a movement, a vibration, a force, a light, whatever it might be, it depends on each one, and they describe this, that it happened like that and came like that, and then this happened and then that, and what does it all mean, all this? Then here one is on the right side. One knows that it is not an imagined experience, that it is a sincere, spontaneous one, and this always has a power of transformation much greater than the experience that was brought about by a mental knowledge.[29]

THE MOTHER

Unceasing Effort for Progress

The delight of victory is sometimes less than the attraction of struggle and suffering; nevertheless the laurel and not the cross should be the aim of the conquering human soul.

Souls that do not aspire are God's failures; but

> Nature is pleased and loves to multiply them because they assure her of stability and prolong her empire.
>
> Those who are poor, ignorant, ill-born or ill-bred are not the common herd; the common herd are all who are satisfied with pettiness and an average humanity.
>
> Help men, but do not pauperise them of their energy; lead and instruct men, but see that their initiative and originality remain intact; take others into thyself, but give them in return the full godhead of their nature. He who can do this is the leader and the guru.
>
> God has made the world a field of battle and filled it with the trampling of combatants and the cries of a great wrestle and struggle. Would you filch His peace without paying the price He has fixed for it?
>
> Distrust a perfect-seeming success, but when having succeeded thou findest still much to do, rejoice and go forward; for the labour is long before the real perfection.
>
> There is no more benumbing error than to mistake a stage for the goal or to linger too long in a resting place. — *Sri Aurobindo*

All that Sri Aurobindo says here is aimed at fighting against human nature with its inertia, its heaviness, laziness, easy satisfactions, hostility to all effort. How many times in life does one meet people who become pacifists because they are afraid to fight, who long for rest before they have earned it, who are satisfied with a little progress and in their imagination and desires make it into a marvellous realisation so as to justify their stopping half-way.

In ordinary life, already, this happens so much. Indeed,

this is the bourgeois ideal, which has deadened mankind and made man into what he is now: "Work while you are young, accumulate wealth, honour, position; be provident, have a little foresight, put something by, lay up a capital, become an official — so that later when you are forty you "can sit down", enjoy your income and later your pension and, as they say, enjoy a well-earned rest." — To sit down, to stop on the way, not to move forward, to go to sleep, to go downhill towards the grave before one's time, cease to live the purpose of life — to sit down!

The minute one stops going forward, one falls back. The moment one is satisfied and no longer aspires, one begins to die. Life is movement, it is effort, it is a march forward, the scaling of a mountain, the climb towards new revelations, towards future realisations. Nothing is more dangerous than wanting to rest. It is in action, in effort, in the march forward that repose must be found, the true repose of complete trust in the divine Grace, of the absence of desires, of victory over egoism.

True repose comes from the widening, the universalisation of the consciousness. Become as vast as the world and you will always be at rest. In the thick of action, in the very midst of the battle, the effort, you will know the repose of infinity and eternity.[30]

THE MOTHER

Freedom from External Influences

Sweet Mother, how can we escape from other people's influence?

By concentrating more and more totally and completely on the Divine. If you aspire with all your ardour, if you want to receive only the divine influence, if all the time you pull back towards yourself what is taken, caught by other influences and with your will put it under the divine influence, you succeed in doing it. It's a work that can't be done in a day, in a minute; you must be vigilant for a very long time, for years; but one can succeed.

First of all you must will it.

For all things, first you must understand, will, and then begin to practise — begin by just a very little. When you catch yourself in the act of doing something because someone else wanted it or because you are not very sure of what you want to do and are in the habit of doing what this one or that one or tradition or customs make you do — because, among the influences under which you live, there are collective suggestions, social traditions, many!... Social habits are something terrible; your consciousness is stuffed with them from the time you are quite small; when a baby you are already told: "This should be done, that should not be done, you must do this in this way, you must not do it in that way", and all that; these are ideas which usually parents or teachers have received in the same way when they were very young and to which they are accustomed and submit by habit; these are the most dangerous influences because they are subtle, they are not expressed outwardly by words; your head was stuffed with them and your feelings and reactions, when you were very small, and it is only later, much later, when you begin to reflect and try to know what the truth is... as soon as you understand that there is something which must be put above all the rest, that there is something which can truly teach you to live, which must form your character, rule your movements... when you understand that, you can look at yourself doing, objectivise yourself, laugh a little at all those multiple small bondages of habit, traditions, the education you have received, and then put the light, consciousness, aspiration for surrender to the Divine on these things, and try to receive the divine inspiration to do things as it's necessary, not according to habits, not according to one's vital impulses, not according to all the vital impulses and personal wills which one receives from others and which push him to do things which perhaps he would not have done without all that.

One must observe all these things, look at them attentively and put them one after another in front of the divine Truth as one can receive it — it is progressive, one receives it purer and purer, stronger and stronger, more and more clear-sightedly — put all these things before it and with an absolute sincerity will that *this* may guide you and nothing else. You do this once, a hundred times, a thousand times, millions of times and after years of sustained effort you can gradually become aware that at last you are a free being — because this is what's remarkable: that when one is perfectly surrendered to the Divine one is perfectly free, and *this is* the absolute condition for freedom, to belong to the Divine alone; you are free from the whole world because you belong only to Him. And this surrender is the supreme liberation, you are also free from your little personal ego and of all things this is the most difficult — and the happiest too, the only thing that can give you a constant peace, an uninterrupted joy and the feeling of an *infinite* freedom from all that afflicts you, dwarfs, diminishes, impoverishes you, and from all that can create the least anxiety in you, the least fear. You are no longer afraid of anything, you no longer fear anything, you are the supreme master of your destiny because it is the Divine who wills in you and guides everything. But this does not happen overnight: a little time and a *great deal* of ardour in the will, not fearing to make any effort and not losing heart when one doesn't succeed, knowing that the victory is certain and that one must last out until it comes.[31]

THE MOTHER

Light and Shadow — Intensification on the Path

When you represent the possibility of a victory, you always have within you the thing contrary to this victory, which is your perpetual trouble.

Each one has his own difficulty.... For instance, a being who must represent fearlessness, courage, you know, a capacity to hold on without giving way before all dangers and all fights, usually somewhere in his being he is a *terrible* coward, and he has to struggle against this almost constantly because this represents the victory he has to win in the world.

It is like a being who ought to be good, full of compassion and generosity; somewhere in his being he is sharp, sour and sometimes even bad; and he has to struggle against this in order to be the other thing. And so on. It goes into *all* the details. It's like that.

And when you see a very black shadow somewhere, *very* black, something that's truly painful, you know, you can be sure that you have in you the possibility of the corresponding light....

In life you are unconscious, you pass all your life in an absolutely vague semi-consciousness, you know nothing about yourself, except just an appearance, nothing more. And you will always be incapable of fulfilling your mission and therefore you do not meet the obstacle in the heart of the difficulty, only an appearance; you are all in the midst of appearances. It's simply that. So your faults are small, your virtues are small, your capacities are mediocre and your difficulties are mediocre, you are entirely mediocre, constantly.

It is only when you begin to walk on the path of Realisation that your possibilities become real, and your difficulties become much greater — quite naturally. Things become intensified.[32]

THE MOTHER

The Only Thing Truly Effective

It is indeed possible even while fasting for very long periods to maintain the full energies and activities of the soul and mind and life, even those of the body, to remain wakeful but concentrated in Yoga all the time, or to think deeply and write day and night, to dispense with

> sleep, to walk eight hours a day, maintaining all these activities separately or together and not feel any loss of strength, any fatigue, any kind of failure or decadence. At the end of the fast one can even resume at once taking the normal or even a greater than the normal amount of nourishment without any transition or precaution such as medical science enjoins, as if both the complete fasting and the feasting were natural conditions, alternating by an immediate and easy passage from one to the other, of a body already trained by a sort of initial transformation to be an instrument of the powers and activities of Yoga....
>
> *Sri Aurobindo*

The description Sri Aurobindo gives here of the possibility of a prolonged fast while maintaining all activities, is a description of his own experience.

He is not speaking of a possibility but of something he has done. But it would be a great mistake to believe that it is an experience that can be imitated in its outer appearance; and even if one managed to do it by an effort of will, it would be perfectly useless from the spiritual point of view, if the experience has not been preceded by a change of consciousness which would be a preliminary liberation.

It is not by abstaining from food that you can make a spiritual progress. It is by being free, not only from all attachment and all desire and preoccupation with food, but even from all need for it; by being in the state in which all these things are so foreign to your consciousness that they have no place there. Only then, as a spontaneous, natural result, can one usefully stop eating. It could be said that the essential condition is to forget to eat — forget, because all the energies of the being and all its concentration are turned towards a more total, more true inner realisation, towards this *constant*, imperative preoccupation with the union of the whole being, including the bodily cells, with the vibration of the divine forces, with the supramental force which is manifesting, so that this may be the true life: not only the purpose of life, but the essence of life, not only an imperative need of life, but all its joy and all its *raison d'être.*

When that is there, when this realisation is attained, then to eat or not to eat, to sleep or not sleep, all this has no longer any importance. It is an outer rhythm left to the play of the universal forces as a whole, finding expression through the circumstances and people around you; and then the body, united, totally united with the inner truth, has a suppleness, a constant adaptability: if food is there, it takes it; if it isn't there, it doesn't think about it. And so too with all things.... This is not life! They are modes of existing to which one adapts oneself without giving it any thought. This gives you the feeling of a kind of blossoming, as a flower opens on a plant, a sort of activity which does not come from a concentrated will but is in harmony with all the forces around you, a way of being which is adapted to the circumstances you live in, which have absolutely no importance in themselves.

There comes a moment when, free from everything, one needs practically nothing, and one can use anything, do anything without this having any real influence on the state of consciousness one is in. This is what really matters. To try through outer gestures or arbitrary decisions which come from a mental consciousness aspiring for a higher life can be a means, not a very effective one but still a sort of reminder to the being that it ought to be something other than what it is in its animality — but it's not that, it's not that at all! A person who could be entirely absorbed in his inner aspiration, to the point of not giving any thought or care to these external things, who would take what comes and not think about it when it doesn't, would be infinitely farther on the path than someone who undertakes ascetic practices with the idea that this will lead him to realisation.

The only thing that is truly effective is the change of consciousness; it is the inner liberation through an intimate, constant union, absolute and inevitable, with the vibration of the supramental forces. The preoccupation of every second, the will of all the elements of the being, the aspiration of the entire being, including all the cells of the body, is this union with the supramental forces, the divine forces. And there is no longer any need at all to be preoccupied with what the consequences will be. What has to be in the play of the universal forces and their manifestation will be, quite naturally, spontaneously, automatically, there is no need to be preoccupied with it. The only thing that matters is the constant, total, complete contact — constant, yes, constant — with the Force, the Light, the Truth, the Power, and that ineffable delight of the supramental consciousness.

That is sincerity. All the rest is an imitation, it is almost a part one plays for oneself.

Perfect purity is *to be*, to be ever more and more, in a self-perfecting becoming. One must never pretend that one *is*: one must *be*, spontaneously.

This is sincerity.[33]

THE MOTHER

Not Renewing a Mistake

To put into practice the little you know is the best way to learn more; it is the most powerful means of advancing on the way — a little bit of really sincere practice. For example, not to do something that you know must not be done. When you have seen a weakness, a disability in your being, you must not allow it to happen again. When, if only for a moment, you have had the vision of what you must be, in an ardent aspiration, you must not — you must never forget to become that.

Some people are always complaining about their disabilities. But that doesn't lead you very far. If, once, you have truly seen your weaknesses and truly, sincerely understood, seen that you must not be like that — that's the end of complaining. Then there is the daily effort, the building up of the will, the vigilance of every moment — you must never allow a recognised mistake to renew itself. To err through ignorance, to err through unconsciousness, is obviously very unfortunate, but it can be put right. Whereas to go on making the same mistake, knowing that it must not be made, is an act of cowardice which we must not permit ourselves.

To say, "Oh, human nature is like this. Oh, we are in the inconscience. Oh, we are in the ignorance" — all this is laziness and weakness. And behind this laziness and weakness there is a huge bad will. There!

I say this because many people have made this remark to me, many. And it is always a way of justifying oneself: "Oh, we are doing what we can." It is not true. Because if you are sincere, once you have seen — as long as you have not seen, nothing can be said — but the moment you see is the moment when you receive the Grace, and once you have received the Grace, you no longer have the right to forget it.[34]

THE MOTHER

Overcoming Hurt Pride

How can we get rid of Abhimana*?**

Oh, good heavens! First of all, see how utterly disastrous it is: it is very petty, it is destructive; and then take a step farther and hold yourself up to ridicule, see to what extent you are ludicrous. So, in this way you get rid of it. But so long as you take it seriously, so long as you justify the movement, so long as somewhere in the mind there's the idea, "After all, it is quite natural, I was ill-treated and I suffer from the ill-treatment", then it is finished, it will never go. But if you begin to understand that it is a sign of weakness, of inferiority — naturally, of a very considerable egoism, a narrow-mindedness, and above all of a pettiness of the feelings, a small-heartedness — if you understand that, you can fight it. But your thought should be in agreement. If there is the attitude, "I have been hurt, I am suffering, I am going to show that I am suffering", then it is like that. I am not going so far as to mention people who nurse a fairly secret spirit of vengeance and say, "I have been made to suffer, I shall make them suffer." This indeed becomes nasty enough for people to notice that it should not exist —

* Hurt pride, self-pity because one feels ill-treated.

though it is not always easy to resist. It indicates something very petty in the nature. It may be very sensitive, it may be very emotional, it may have a certain intensity but it is quite petty, it is all turned back on oneself, and is quite petty.

Of course, you can use your reason, if you have one which works. You can make use of the reason and can tell yourself something which is very true: that in our being it is only egoism which always suffers, and that if there was no egoism there would be no suffering, and that if one wants the spiritual life, one must overcome his egoism. So the first thing to do is to look straight at this suffering, perceive to what an extent it is the expression of a very petty egoism and then sweep the place clean, make a clean ground and say, "I don't want this dirt, I am going to clean my inner chamber."[35]

THE MOTHER

The Impossible

> What I cannot do now is the sign of what I shall do hereafter. The sense of impossibility is the beginning of all possibilities. Because this temporal universe was a paradox and an impossibility, therefore the Eternal created it out of His being. —*Sri Aurobindo*

Do you know why this seems paradoxical to you? It is simply because Sri Aurobindo has not put in the guide marks of the thought, hasn't led you step by step from one thought to another. It is nothing else. It is almost elementary in its simplicity.

And I am simply going to ask you a question — but in fact I expect no answer — to tell you something very simple: When does something seem impossible to you? — It is when you try to do it. If you had never tried to do it, it would never have seemed impossible to you.

And how is it that you tried to do it? — Because it was somewhere in your consciousness. If it had not been in your consciousness, you would not have tried to do it; and the moment it is in your consciousness, it is quite obvious that it is something you will realise. That alone which is not in your consciousness you cannot realise. It's as simple as that!

Only, instead of telling you the thing in this way, Sri Aurobindo puts it in a way that stimulates your thought. That is the virtue of paradoxes, they compel you to think.

Then, Sweet Mother, what does "impossible" mean?

There is nothing impossible in the world except what is outside your consciousness. And as your consciousness can grow, as what is not in your consciousness today may be in your consciousness after some time, for the consciousness can become wider, so in the eternity of time nothing is impossible.

At the present moment... , at a given moment, in certain circumstances, there are impossibilities. But from the eternal point of view in the infinity of time, nothing, nothing is impossible. And the proof is that everything will be. All things, not only those which are conceivable at present, but all those which at present are inconceivable, all things are not only possible, but will be realised. For what we call the Eternal, the Infinite, the Supreme, the Absolute — we give him many names, but in fact He is eternal, infinite, absolute — contains in himself not only all that is, but also all that will be, eternally, infinitely; and therefore nothing is impossible. Only, for the consciousness of the temporal and objective being, all things are not possible at the same time; it is necessary to conceive of space and time to make them possible. But outside the manifestation, *everything* is, simultaneously, eternally, potentially, in its possibility. And it is this All, inconceivable, for He is not manifest, who manifests in order to become conceivable....

But if we go back to the beginning, then it becomes extremely practical, concrete and very encouraging.... For we say this: in order to have the idea of the impossible, that something is "impossible", you must attempt it. For example, if at this moment you feel that what I am telling you is impossible to understand (*laughing*), this means that you are trying to understand it; and if you try to understand it, this means it is within your consciousness, otherwise you could not try to understand it — just as I am in your consciousness, just as my words are in your consciousness, just as what Sri Aurobindo has written is also in your consciousness, otherwise you would have no contact with it. But for the moment it is impossible to understand, for want of a few small cells in the brain, nothing else, it is very simple. And as these cells develop through attention, concentration and effort, when you have listened attentively and made an effort to understand, well, after a few hours or a few days or a few months, new convolutions will be formed in your brain, and all this will become quite natural. You will wonder how there could have been a time when you did not understand: "It is so simple!" But so long as these convolutions are not there, you may make an effort, you may even give yourself a headache, but you will not understand.

It is very encouraging because, fundamentally, the only thing necessary is to want it and to have the necessary patience. What is incomprehensible for you today will be quite clear in a short time. And note that it is not necessary that you should give yourself a headache every day and at every minute by trying to understand! One very simple thing is enough: to listen as well as you can, to have a sort of will or aspiration or, you might even say, desire to understand, and then that's all. You make a little opening in your consciousness to let the thing enter; and your aspiration makes this opening, like a tiny notch inside, a little hole somewhere in what is shut up, and then you let the thing enter. It will work. And it will build up in your brain the elements necessary to express itself. You no longer need to think about it. You try to understand something else, you work, study, reflect, think about all sorts of things; and then after a few months — or perhaps a year, perhaps less, perhaps more — you open the book once again and read the same sentence, and it seems as clear as crystal to you! Simply because what was necessary for understanding has been built up in your brain.[36]

THE MOTHER

Progress on the Path

Sweet Mother, when we make an effort to do better but don't see any progress, we feel discouraged. What is the best thing to do?

Not to be discouraged! Despondency leads nowhere.

To begin with, the first thing to tell yourself is that you are almost entirely incapable of knowing whether you are making progress or not, for very often what seems to us to be a state of stagnation is a long — sometimes long, but in any case not endless — preparation for a leap forward. We sometimes seem to be marking time for weeks or months, and then suddenly something that was being prepared makes its appearance, and we see that there is quite a considerable change and *on several points* at a time.

As with everything in yoga, the effort for progress must be made for the love of the effort for progress. The joy of effort, the aspiration for progress must be enough in themselves, quite independent of the result. Everything one does in yoga must be done for the joy of doing it, and not in view of the result one wants to obtain.... Indeed, in life, always, in all things, the result does not belong to us. And if we want to keep the right attitude, we must act, feel, think, strive spontaneously, for *that* is what we must do, and not in view of the result to be obtained.

As soon as we think of the result we begin to bargain and that takes away all sincerity from the effort. You make an effort to progress because you feel within you the need, the *imperative* need to make an effort and progress; and this effort is the gift you offer to the Divine Consciousness in you, the Divine Consciousness in the Universe, it is your way of expressing your gratitude, offering your self; and whether this results in progress or not is of no importance. You will progress when it is decided that the time has come to progress and not because you desire it.

If you wish to progress, if you make an effort to control

yourself for instance, to overcome certain defects, weaknesses, imperfections, and if you expect to get a more or less immediate result from your effort, your effort loses all sincerity, it becomes a bargaining. You say, "See! I am going to make an effort, but that's because I want this in exchange for my effort." You are no longer spontaneous, no longer natural.

So there are two things to remember. First, we are incapable of judging *what* the result ought to be. If we put our trust in the Divine, if we say... if we say, "Well now, I am going to give everything, everything, all I can give, effort, concentration, and *He* will judge what has to be given in exchange or even whether anything should be given in exchange, and I do not know what the result should be." Before we transform anything in ourselves, are we quite sure of the direction, the way, the form that this transformation should take? — Not at all. So, it is only our imagination and usually we greatly limit the result to be obtained and make it altogether petty, mean, superficial, relative. We do not know what the result can truly be, what it ought to be. We know it later. When it comes, when the change takes place, then if we look back, we say, "Ah! that's it, that is what I was moving towards" — but we know it only later. Before that we only have vague imaginations which are quite superficial and childish in comparison with the true progress, the true transformation.

So we say, first point: we have an aspiration but we don't really know the true result we ought to obtain. Only the Divine can know that.

And secondly, if we tell the Divine, "I am giving you my effort, but, you know, in exchange I must make progress, otherwise I won't give you anything at all!"— that is bargaining. That's all.[37]

THE MOTHER

The True Reason

Those who want to follow the true path will naturally be exposed to the attacks of all the forces of ill-will, which not only do not understand but generally hate what they do not understand.

If you are troubled, vexed, even discouraged by all the spiteful stupidities that people may say about you, you will not be able to advance much on the way. And these things come to you not because you are unlucky or because your lot is not a happy one, but because on the contrary the divine Consciousness and Grace take your resolution seriously and allow circumstances to become the touchstones on the way, to see if your resolution is sincere and you are strong enough to face the difficulties.

Therefore, if someone laughs at you, or says something which is not kind, the first thing to do is to look within yourself and see what is the weakness or imperfection which has allowed such a thing to happen, and not to be disconsolate or indignant or sad because people do not appreciate you for what you consider to be your proper value; on the contrary, you should thank the divine Grace for having pointed out to you the weakness or imperfection or deformation that you have to rectify.

So instead of being unhappy, you can be fully satisfied and take advantage, a great advantage, of the harm that someone wanted to do to you.

Besides, if you truly wish to follow the path and to do the yoga, you should not do it so that people will appreciate and honour you; you should do it because it is an imperative need of your being and because you can be happy only in that way. Whether people appreciate you or do not appreciate you has absolutely no importance whatever. You can tell yourself beforehand that the farther you are from the ordinary man, the more foreign to the way of the ordinary creature, the less you will be appreciated — quite naturally, for they will not understand you. And I repeat that this has no importance whatever.

True sincerity consists in following the way because you cannot do otherwise, in consecrating yourself to the divine life because you cannot do otherwise, in endeavouring to transform your being and emerge into the Light because you cannot do otherwise, because it is the very reason for which you live.

When it is like that, you can be sure that you are on the right path.[38]

THE MOTHER

Spontaneity

I suppose most of you come on Fridays to listen to the reading of *Wu Wei*. If you have listened, you will remember that something's said there about being "spontaneous", and that the true way of living the true life is to live spontaneously.

What Lao Tse calls spontaneous is this: instead of being moved by a personal will — mental, vital or physical — one ought to stop all outer effort and let oneself be guided and moved by what the Chinese call *Tao*, which they identify with the Godhead — or God or the Supreme Principle or the Origin of all things or the creative Truth, indeed all possible human notions of the Divine and the goal to be attained.

To be spontaneous means not to think out, organise, decide and make an effort to realise with the personal will.

I am going to give you two examples to make you understand what true spontaneity is. One — you all know about it undoubtedly — is of the time Sri Aurobindo began writing the *Arya*,* in 1914. It was neither a mental knowledge nor even a mental creation which he transcribed: he silenced his mind and sat at the typewriter, and from above, from the higher planes, all that had to be written came down, all ready, and he had only to move his fingers on the typewriter and it was transcribed. It was in this state of mental silence which allows the knowledge — and even the expression — from above to pass through that he wrote the whole *Arya*, with its sixty-four printed pages a month. This is why, besides, he could do it, for if it had been a mental work of construction it would have been quite impossible.

That is true mental spontaneity.

And if one carries this a little further, one should never think and plan beforehand what one ought to say or write.

* It was in the review *Arya*, within a period of six years (1914-1920), that Sri Aurobindo published most of his major works: *The Life Divine, The Synthesis of Yoga, The Human Cycle* (originally *The Psychology of Social Development*),*The Ideal of Human Unity, Essays on the Gita, The Secret of the Veda, The Future Poetry, The Foundations of Indian Culture* (originally a number of series under other titles).

One should simply be able to silence one's mind, to turn it like a receptacle towards the higher Consciousness and express as it receives it, in mental silence, what comes from above. That would be true spontaneity.

Naturally, this is not very easy, it asks for preparation.

And if one comes down to the sphere of action, it is still more difficult; for normally, if one wants to act with some kind of logic, one usually has to think out beforehand what one wants to do and plan it before doing it, otherwise one may be tossed about by all sorts of desires and impulses which would be very far from the inspiration spoken about in *Wu Wei*; it would simply be movements of the lower nature driving you to act. Therefore, unless one has reached the state of wisdom and detachment of the Chinese sage mentioned in this story, it is better not to be spontaneous in one's daily actions, for one would risk being the plaything of all the most disorderly impulses and influences.[39]

THE MOTHER

Spontaneity in Aspiration

Mother, when we make an effort, there's something in us which becomes very self-satisfied and boastful and contented with this effort, and that spoils everything. Then how can we get rid of this?

Ah, that's what looks on at what it is doing! There is always someone who observes when one is doing something. Now sometimes, he becomes proud. Obviously, this takes away much strength from the effort. I think it is that: it is the habit of looking at oneself acting, looking at oneself living. It is necessary to observe oneself but I think it is still more necessary to try to be absolutely sincere and spontaneous, very spontaneous in what one does: not always to go on observing oneself, looking at what one is doing, judging oneself — sometimes severely. In fact it is almost as bad as patting oneself with satisfaction, the two are equally bad. One should be so sincere in his aspiration that he doesn't even know he is aspiring, that he becomes the aspiration itself. When this indeed can be realised, one truly attains to an extraordinary power.

One minute, one minute of this, and you can prepare years of realisation. When one is no longer a self-regarding being, an ego looking at itself acting, when one becomes the action itself, above all in the aspiration, this truly is good. When there is no longer a person who is aspiring, when it is an aspiration which leaps up with a fully concentrated impulsion, then truly it goes very far. Otherwise there is always mixed up in it a little vanity, a little self-complacency, a little self-pity also, all kinds of little things which come and spoil everything. But it is difficult.[40]

THE MOTHER

In Difficulty — Learning to be Quiet

From the point of view of individual development and for those who are still at the beginning of the path, to know how to remain silent before what one does not understand is one of the things which would help most in the progress — to know how to remain silent, not only externally, without uttering a word, but also to know how to be silent within, so that the mind does not assert its ignorance with its usual presumptuousness, does not try to understand with an instrument that is incapable of understanding, that it may know its own weakness and open simply, quietly, waiting until the time has come for it to receive the light, because only the Light, the true Light, can give it understanding. It is not all that it has learnt nor all that it has observed nor all its so-called experience of life, it is something else which is completely beyond it. And until this something else — which is the expression of the Grace — manifests within it, if, very quietly, very modestly the mind remains silent and does not try to understand and, above all, to judge, things would go *much* faster.

The noise made by all the words, all the ideas in your head is so deafening that it prevents you from hearing the truth when it wants to manifest.

To learn to be quiet and silent... When you have a problem to solve, instead of turning over in your head all the possibilities, all the consequences, all the possible things one should or should not do, if you remain quiet with an aspiration for goodwill, if possible a need for goodwill, the solution comes very quickly. And as you are silent you are able to hear it.

When you are caught in a difficulty, try this method: instead of becoming agitated, turning over all the ideas and actively seeking solutions, of worrying, fretting, running here and there inside your head — I don't mean externally, for externally you probably have enough common sense not to do that! but inside, in your head — *remain quiet.* And according to your nature, with ardour or peace, with intensity or widening or with all these together, implore the Light and wait for it to come.

In this way the path would be considerably shortened.[41]

THE MOTHER

In Difficulty — Widening Oneself

What do you mean by these words: "When you are in difficulty, widen yourself"?

I am speaking, of course, of difficulties on the path of yoga, incomprehension, limitations, things like obstacles, which prevent you from advancing. And when I say "widen yourself", I mean widen your consciousness.

Difficulties always arise from the ego, that is, from your more or less egoistic personal reaction to circumstances, events and people around you, to the conditions of your life. They also come from that feeling of being closed up in a sort of shell, which prevents your consciousness from uniting with higher and vaster realities.

One may very well *think* that one wants to be vast, wants to be universal, that all is the expression of the Divine, that one must have no egoism — one may think all sorts of things — but that is not necessarily a cure, for very often one knows what one ought to do, and yet one doesn't do it, for one reason or another.

But if, when you have to face anguish, suffering, revolt, pain or a feeling of helplessness — whatever it may be, all the things that come to you on the path and which precisely are your difficulties — if physically, that is to say, in your body-consciousness, you can have the feeling of widening yourself, one could say of unfolding yourself — you feel as it were all folded up, one fold on another like a piece of cloth which is folded and refolded and folded again — so if you have this feeling that what is holding and strangling you and making you suffer or paralysing your movement, is like a too closely, too tightly folded piece of cloth or like a parcel that is too well-tied, too well-packed, and that slowly, gradually, you undo all the folds and stretch yourself out exactly as one unfolds a piece of cloth or a sheet of paper and spreads it out flat, and you lie flat and make yourself very wide, as wide as possible, spreading yourself out as far as you can, opening yourself and stretching out in an attitude of complete passivity with what I could call "the face to the light": not curling back upon your difficulty, doubling up on it, shutting it in, so to say, into yourself, but, on the contrary, unfurling yourself as much as you can, as perfectly as you can, putting the difficulty before the Light — the Light which comes from above — if you do that in all the domains, and even if mentally you don't succeed in doing it — for it is sometimes difficult — if you can imagine yourself doing this *physically*, almost materially, well, when you have finished unfolding yourself and stretching yourself out, you will find that more than three-quarters of the difficulty is gone. And then just a little work of receptivity to the Light and the last quarter will disappear.

This is much easier than struggling against a difficulty with one's thought, for if you begin to discuss with yourself, you will find that there are arguments for and against which are so convincing that it is quite impossible to get out of it without a higher light. Here, you do not struggle against the difficulty, you do not try to convince yourself; ah! you simply stretch out in the Light as though you lay stretched on the sands in the sun. And you let the Light do its work.[42]

THE MOTHER

Leaving the Path

When one draws back from the path, one draws back for the present life or...

In this, you see, there are many different cases, and they depend on the nature of the drawing back. If it is a small set-back or a small halt, you can start again. But it is ten times more difficult than before.

Why?

Why? Because it is so. Because you have accumulated obstacles in yourself by your cowardice and weakness. All those difficulties which you must conquer are like spiritual tests which you have to pass. And if you fail in your test, well, the next one will be much more difficult. This is the general occult law. One can't escape it. If you are faced with making an effort and making progress, if you fail... And note that in the present conditions you are not warned beforehand, which makes the test much more difficult to pass. In former days, the days of old, the candidates were told, "Now, prepare yourself. You are going to undergo terrible trials: you will be enclosed in a coffin, you will have to face terrible dangers. But these are tests to find out if you have the necessary qualities." A man forewarned, you understand, is as good as ten, as we say. Once they were warned that it was a trial, they did not take it seriously and it was much easier.

But that's no longer the practice. This is no longer done. It is life itself, the circumstances of each day which are the trials through which you have to pass. Some people instinctively feel that they are facing a decision that's to be taken, a special effort that's to be made, and they make this effort within themselves and cross the step. These acquire a much greater strength to cross the next step. When one has gained a small victory over his lower being, the next time he has a much greater strength to take the next step. On the contrary, if one is blind, ignorant, stupid or ill-willed and, instead of saying "yes" to the trial that faces him, he revolts or refuses it, then, you see, this is expressed by: "One has not passed his test, one has failed in his test." But the next time, one is compelled not only to make an effort to conquer this, but to make a still greater effort to redress the wrong one has done to himself. So it is much more difficult.

But these things happen to everyone on the path, all the time, perhaps even daily. There are small things, there are things a little bigger. The small ones one can turn, you see, by chance the right way. For the big ones one must first have a kind of instinct. One must pay attention and do the right thing in the right way. But there are other things still. When one is at a critical moment of his development, and it is absolutely necessary to cross the step in order to go forward — at that moment, there are always two possibilities: that of crossing the step, and then one immediately makes a terrific progress; or else to become slack, and then this indeed is more than a halt, even more than a set-back, it can be a very serious fall into a chasm. There are abysses from which one does not come up again; and so, in this case it means a life lost.

But if one has within, besides the part that has given way and fallen, if somewhere one has a very ardent flame, if one is ready for anything, all possible suffering, all possible effort, all possible sacrifices to redress what one has done, in order to climb back from the bottom of the abyss, to find the path again, one can do it. This flame has the power to call the Grace. And with the Grace there is nothing impossible. But it must be a real flame, something very powerful, because when one is at the bottom of the hole it is not easy to come out of it. Between the first kind, which is simply a little halt on the way and which makes the next step just a little more difficult, and the last one I am speaking about, there are many degrees; and so one can't say that if one leaves the path it is for a lifetime. That would be only an extreme case.

But if one leaves the path, it is even very difficult to find it again. What is strange is that in leaving it one loses it. There are legends of this kind in all countries: of people who have left the path and then later searched for it and never found it again. It was as if it had vanished. They lost it and this truly is a very sad thing.

But when you are on the path, I said this — I was just saying it — when you are on the path, do not ever leave it. Wait a little, you can hesitate as long as you want before taking it; but the minute you set your foot on it, it is finished, don't leave it. Because this has consequences which can even extend to several lives. It is something very serious. That is why, besides, I never push anyone to take the path. You are quite a number of children here; I have never asked anyone — only those who came to me and told me, "I want it." And to these also, unless I am absolutely sure of them because it is written in their destiny that they have come for that, I always say, "Think about it, think, be quite sure that this is what you want and nothing else." And when they have reflected and decided, it is finished. One should no longer move away, one should go straight to the end. I mean, one should not leave the path any more. One should go forward at all costs and try not to stop too often on the way, because it is easier to continue even if it is hard, you see, than to begin all over again when one has stopped. A much greater effort is needed to get going again than to continue on the way. And you see, logically I should not say it, but I have already warned all who are here, I have told them, "Don't ever take lightly all the circumstances of each day, all the tiny little things of life, all the small events, you know; never take all this lightly." Never react with your lower being. Each time you are told to do something or not to do it — you are not told this very often, but each time you are told, before reacting think a little, try to find in yourself the part which reacts. Do not react just like that with what is most commonplace in you. Enter within yourself, try to find the best in yourself and with this you must react. *It is very important, it is very important.*

There are people who mark time for years because they haven't done this. There are others who seem to fly, so fast do they go, because they pay attention to this. And those who don't do that throw the blame always on the Divine. They accuse the Grace. They tell her, "It is You who deceived me, it is You who put me into difficulty, it is You who made me stumble, it is You who are a monster", not exactly in these words, but their thought is like this. And so, naturally, they make their case worse because they push away even the help they could have had in their difficulty. There we are.

I could tell you many more things, but it will come gradually. In any case, if you can keep within yourself a confidence, a candid trust which does not argue, and the sense of... yes, it is truly a kind of trust that what is done for you, in spite of all appearances, is always the best thing to lead you in the quickest way possible out of all your difficulties and towards the goal... if you can keep that strong in you, well, your path will become tremendously easier.

You will tell me that it is very difficult to keep it, but children keep it very well. They must have truly come upon particularly detestable parents to lose it; but if their parents are simply good enough, they keep this very well. Well, it is this attitude; if you can tell yourself, "Good, perhaps the divine Grace deserves our confidence", simply this, nothing else, you will avoid many difficulties, many. In fact this avoids many difficulties even in ordinary life, and many worries.[43]

THE MOTHER

7. EXPERIENCES ON THE PATH

How to Have the Experience

We read, we try to understand, we explain, we try to know. But a single minute of true experience teaches us more than millions of words and hundreds of explanations.

So the first question is: "How to have the experience?"

To go within yourself, that is the first step.

And then, once you have succeeded in going within yourself deeply enough to feel the reality of that which is within, to widen yourself progressively, systematically, to become as vast as the universe and lose the sense of limitation.

These are the first two preparatory movements.

And these two things must be done in the greatest possible calm, peace and tranquillity. This peace, this tranquillity brings about silence in the mind and stillness in the vital.

This effort, this attempt must be renewed very regularly, persistently. And after a certain lapse of time, which may be longer or shorter, you begin to perceive a reality that is different from the reality perceived in the ordinary, external consciousness.

Naturally, by the action of Grace, the veil may suddenly be rent from within, and at once you can enter the true truth; but even when that happens, in order to obtain the full value and full effect of the experience, you must maintain yourself in a state of inner receptivity, and to do that, it is indispensable for you to go within each day.[44]

THE MOTHER

Sweet Mother, if there is someone who wants to have experiences or something like that, what is the first thing he should do?

To have experiences? What kind of experiences? Have visions or have psychological experiences or — what kind of experiences?

In fact, the whole life is an experience, isn't it? We spend our time having experiences. You mean having a contact with other realities than physical ones? Is it that? Ah!

Well, I think the first condition is to have, to begin with, the faith that there is something other than the physical reality. This can be the first condition. Then the second condition is to try to find what it is, and the best field of action is oneself. So one must begin by studying oneself a little, and manage to discern between what depends exclusively on the body and what on something else which is not the body. One can begin like that. One can begin by observing one's feelings or thoughts in their working; because... sensations are so linked to the body that it is very difficult to distinguish them, they are so tied to our senses, and the senses are instruments of the body, so it is difficult to discern. But feelings already escape... the feelings one experiences; and to try to find the root of this... and then the thoughts... What are thoughts?

If one begins to find out, to understand what a feeling is and what a thought is, and how it works, then one can already go quite far on the path with that. One must at the same time observe how his feelings and thoughts have an action on the body, what the reciprocity is. And then, there is another exercise which consists in looking into oneself for what is persistent, what is lasting, something which makes one say "I", and which is not the body. For obviously, when one was very small, and then when each year one grows up, if one takes fairly long distances, for example a distance of about ten years, they are very different "I"s from what one was when as small as this (*gesture*), and then what one is now; it is difficult to say that it is the same person, you see. If one takes only this, still there is something which has the feeling of always being the same person. So one must reflect, seek, try to understand what it is. This indeed can lead you far on the path. Then if one also studies the relation between these different things — between thoughts, feelings, their action on the body, the reciprocal action of the body on these things — and also what it is that says "I" permanently, what it is that can trace a curve in the movement of the being, if one seeks carefully enough, it leads you quite far. Naturally if one seeks far enough and with enough persistence, one reaches the psychic.

It is the path to lead you to the psychic; and so this is the experience, it is the first experience. When one has the contact with the permanent part of one's immortal being, through this immortality one can go still further and reach the Eternal. It is still another state of consciousness. But it is in this way that one follows the path, gradually. There are other ways, but this is the one which is always within reach. You see, one always has his body with him, and his feelings and thoughts, and at any moment of the day whatever, even in the night one can be busy with this; while if one must have something else around him, people or things or certain conditions, it is more complicated; but this is always there within one's reach. Nobody can prevent you from having your body with you, your thought and your feelings, your sensations; it is the field of work which is always there, it is very convenient — no need to seek outside. One has all that is necessary. And so what must be acquired is the power of observation and the capacity for concentrating and for pursuing a little continuously a certain movement in one's being; as when you have some very strong feeling which takes hold of you, seizes you, then you must look at it, so to say, and concentrate upon it and manage to find out where it comes from, what has brought you this. Just this work of concentrating in order to succeed in finding this out is enough to lead you straight to an experience. And then if, for example, you want to do something practical, if in your feelings you are completely upset, agitated, if there's a kind of storm within, then by concentrating you can try to find out the cause of all that, you see, the inner cause, the real cause, and at the same time you can aspire to bring peace, quietude, a kind of inner immobility into your feelings, because without that you can't see clearly. When everything is in a whirlwind one sees nothing; as when you are in a great tempest and the wind is blowing from all sides and there are clouds of dust, you cannot see; it is the same thing. To be able to see, all must become quiet. So you must aspire and then draw into this storm... draw peace, quietude, immobility, like this; and then if you succeed it is still another experience, it is the beginning.

Of course one can sit down and try... not to meditate, because that's an activity of thought which does not lead to experience, but to concentrate and aspire and open oneself to the force from above; and if one does it persistently enough, there is a moment when one feels this force, this peace or this silence, this quietude descending, penetrating and descending into the being quite far. The first day it may be very little, and then gradually it becomes more. This also is an experience. All these are easy things to do.

But if, for example, one has a dream, when one remembers it very precisely in its details and concentrates in order to understand this dream, this too can be an experience, some door of understanding can open and one may suddenly get the deep meaning which was hidden behind the dream; this also is an experience — many things... and one always has the opportunity to have them. Of course the experience which most gives you the sense of a revelation or of something new is the one you have as soon as you enter into contact with the psychic, and in the psychic, when you are in the presence of the Divine; this indeed is the typal experience, the one which has an action on the whole orientation and activity of the being. But it may come quickly or may also take time. Yet between the state in which one is at present and that state there are many rungs. I mean these are rungs of experiences one can have.

So it is a vast programme. The first steps are these: to collect oneself, try to be very quiet and see what is happening within, the relations between things, and what is happening inside, not just live only on the surface.[45]

THE MOTHER

Work — A School of Experience

If you don't do anything, you cannot have any experience. The whole life is a field of experience. Each movement you make, each thought you have, each work you do, can be an experience, and *must be* an experience; and naturally work in particular is a field of experience where one must apply all the progress which one endeavours to make inwardly.

If you remain in meditation or contemplation without working, well, you don't know if you have progressed or not. You may live in an illusion, the illusion of your progress; while if you begin to work, all the circumstances of your work, the contact with others, the material occupation, all this is a field of experience in order that you may become aware not only of the progress made but of all the progress that remains to be made. If you live closed up in yourself, without acting, you may live in a completely subjective illusion; the moment you externalise your action and enter into contact with others, with circumstances and the objects of life, you become aware absolutely objectively of whether you have made progress or not, whether you are more calm, more conscious, stronger, more unselfish, whether you no longer have any desire, any preference, any weakness, any unfaithfulness — you can become aware of all this by working. But if you remain enclosed in a meditation that's altogether personal, you may enter into a total illusion and never come out of it, and believe that you have realised extraordinary things, while really you have only the impression, the illusion that you have done so.[46]

THE MOTHER

Understanding through Experience

... to really understand what it means, one feels that philosophy is always skirting the truth, like a tangent that draws closer and closer but never touches — that there is something that escapes. And this something is in truth everything.

To understand these things... there is only experience — *to live* this truth, not to feel it in the way the ordinary senses do but to realise within oneself the truth, the concrete existence of both states, simultaneously, existing together even while they are opposite conditions. All words can lead only to confusion; only experience gives the tangible reality of the *thing*: the simultaneous existence of the Absolute and the relativities, of Oneness and multiplicity, not as two states following each other and one resulting from the other, but as a state which can be perceived in two opposite ways depending on... the position one takes in relation to the Reality.

Words in themselves falsify the experience. To speak in words one must take not a step backwards but a step downwards, and the essential truth escapes. One must use them simply as a more or less accessible path to reach the *thing* itself which cannot be formulated. And from this point of view no formulation is better than any other; the best of all is the one that helps each one to remember, that is, the way in which the intervention of the Grace has crystallised in the thought.

Probably no two ways are identical, everyone must find his own. But one must not be mistaken, it is not "finding" by reasoning, it is "finding" by aspiration; it is not by study and analysis, but by the intensity of the aspiration and the sincerity of the inner opening.

When one is truly and exclusively turned to the spiritual Truth, whatever name may be given to it, when all the rest becomes secondary, when that alone is imperative and inevitable, then, *one single moment* of intense, absolute, total concentration is enough to receive the answer.

The experience comes first, in this case, and it is only later, as a consequence and a memory that the formulation becomes clear. In this way one is sure not to make a mistake. The formulation may be more or less exact, that is of no importance, so long as one doesn't make a dogma out of it.

It is good for you, that is all that is needed. If you want to impose it on others, whatever it may be, even if it is perfect in itself, it becomes false.

That is why religions are always mistaken — always — because they want to standardise the expression of an experience and impose it on everyone as an irrefutable truth. The experience was true, complete in itself, convincing — for the one who had it. The formulation he made of it was excellent — for himself. But to want to impose it on others is a fundamental error which has altogether disastrous consequences, always, which always leads far, very far from the Truth.

That is why all the religions, however beautiful they may be, have always led man to the worst excesses. All the crimes, the horrors perpetrated in the name of religion are among the darkest stains on human history, and simply because of this little initial error: wanting what is true for one individual to be true for the mass or collectivity.

(*Silence*)

The path must be shown and the doors opened but everyone must *follow* the path, pass through the doors and go towards his personal realisation.

The only help one can and should receive is that of the Grace which formulates itself in everyone according to his own need.[47]

THE MOTHER

Spontaneity and Experience

... once one enters the yoga and wants to do yoga, it is very necessary not to be the toy of one's own mental formations. If one wants to rely on one's experiences, one must take great care not to construct within oneself the notion of the experiences one wants to have, the idea one has about them, the form one expects or hopes to see. For, the mental formation, as I already have told you very often, is a real formation, a real creation, and with your idea you create forms which are to a certain extent independent of you and return to you as though from outside and give you the impression of being experiences. But these experiences which are either willed or sought after or expected are not spontaneous experiences and risk being illusions — at times even dangerous illusions.

Therefore, when you follow a mental discipline, you must be particularly careful not to imagine or want to have certain experiences, for in this way you can create for yourself the illusion of these experiences. In the domain of yoga, this very strict and severe spontaneity is *absolutely* indispensable.

For that, naturally, one must not have any ambition or desire or excessive imagination or what I call "spiritual romanticism", the taste for the miraculous — all this ought to be very carefully eliminated so as to be sure of advancing fearlessly.[48]

THE MOTHER

Getting the Full Benefit from an Experience

... the experience precedes and transcends by far the formulation you give it in your mind. The experience comes before, often long before the capacity to formulate it. The experience has a fullness, a force, a power of *direct* action on the nature, which is immediate, instantaneous. Let us take as an example that in certain circumstances or by an exceptional grace you are suddenly put into contact with a supramental light, power or consciousness. It is like an abrupt opening in your closed shell, like a rent in that opaque envelope which separates you from the Truth, and the contact is established. Immediately this force, this consciousness, this light acts, even on your physical cells; it acts in the mind, in the vital, in the body, changes the vibrations, organises the substance and begins its work of transformation. You are under the impact of this sudden contact and action; for you it is a sort of indescribable, inexpressible state which takes hold of you, you haven't any clear, precise, definite idea of it, it is... "something that happens". It may give you the impression of being wonderful or tremendous, but it is inexpressible and incomprehensible for you. That is the experience in its essence and its true power.

Gradually, as the action is prolonged and the outer being begins to assimilate this action, there awakens a capacity of observation, first in the mental consciousness, and a kind of objectivisation occurs: something in the mind looks on, observes and translates in its own way. This is what you call understanding, and this is what gives you the impression (*smiling*) that you are having an experience. But that is already considerably diminished in comparison with the experience itself, it is a transcription adapted to your mental, vital and physical dimension, that is, something that is shrunken, hardened—and it gives you at the same time the impression that it is growing clearer; that is to say, it has become as limited as your understanding.

That is a phenomenon which always occurs even in the best cases. I am not speaking of those instances where this power of experience is absorbed by the unconsciousness of your being and expressed by a more and more unconscious movement; I am speaking of the case in which your mind is clear, your aspiration clear, and where you have already advanced quite considerably on the path.... And even when your mind begins to be transformed, when it is used to receiving this Light, when it can be penetrated by it, is sufficiently receptive to absorb it, the moment it wants to express it in a way understandable to the human consciousness—I don't mean the ordinary consciousness but even the enlightened human consciousness—the moment it wants to formulate, to make it precise and understandable, it reduces, diminishes, limits — it attenuates, weakens, blurs the experience, even granting that it is pure enough not to falsify it. For if, anywhere in the being, in the mind or the vital, there is some insincerity which is tolerated, well, then the experience is completely falsified and deformed. But I am speaking of the best instances, where the being is sincere, under control, and where it functions most favourably: the formulation in words which are understandable by the human mind is *necessarily*, inevitably, a restriction, a diminution of the power of action of the experience. When you can tell yourself clearly and consciously: "This and that and the other happened", when you can describe the phenomenon comprehensibly, it has already lost some of its power of action, its intensity, its truth and force. But this does not mean that the intensity, the power of action and the force were not there — they were there, and probably in the best cases the utmost effect of the experience is produced before you begin to give it a comprehensible form.

I am speaking here of the best cases. I am not speaking of the innumerable cases of those who begin to have an experience and whose mind becomes curious, wakes up and says, "Oh! what is happening?" Then everything vanishes. Or maybe one catches the deformed tail of something which has lost all its force and all its reality.... The first thing to do is to teach your mind *not to stir*: "Above all, don't move! Above all, don't move, let the thing develop fully without wanting to know what is happening; don't be stupid, keep quiet, be still, and wait. Your turn will always come too soon, never too late." It should be possible to live an experience for hours and for days together without feeling the need to formulate it to yourself. When one does that, one gets the full benefit from it. Then it works, it churns the nature, it transforms the cells — it begins its real work of transformation. But as soon as you begin to look and to understand and to formulate, it is already something that belongs to the past.[49]

THE MOTHER

8. THE GUIDE, THE HELPER, THE LORD DIVINE

Certitudes

In the deep there is a greater deep, in the heights a greater height. Sooner shall man arrive at the borders of infinity than at the fullness of his own being. For that being is infinity, is God.

I aspire to infinite force, infinite knowledge, infinite bliss. Can I attain it? Yes, but the nature of infinity is that it has no end. Say not therefore that I attain it. I become it. Only so can man attain God by becoming God.

But before attaining he can enter into relations with him. To enter into relations with God is Yoga, the highest rapture & the noblest utility. There are relations within the compass of the humanity we have developed. These are called prayer, worship, adoration, sacrifice, thought, faith, science, philosophy. There are other relations beyond our developed capacity, but within the compass of the humanity we have yet to develop. Those are the relations that are attained by the various practices we usually call Yoga.

We may not know him as God, we may know him as Nature, our Higher Self, Infinity, some ineffable goal. It was so that Buddha approached Him; so approaches him the rigid Adwaitin. He is accessible even to the Atheist. To the materialist He disguises Himself in matter. For the Nihilist he waits ambushed in the bosom of Annihilation.

*Ye yathā mām prppadyante tānstathaiva bhajāmyaham.**[50]

SRI AUROBINDO

The Divine — A Certitude of Experience

I will begin not with doubt but with the demand for the Divine as a concrete certitude, quite as concrete as any physical phenomenon caught by the senses. Now, certainly, the Divine must be such a certitude not only as concrete but more concrete than anything sensed by ear or eye or touch in the world of Matter; but it is a certitude not of mental thought but of essential experience. When the Peace of God descends on you, when the Divine Presence is there within you, when the Ananda rushes on you like a sea, when you are driven like a leaf before the wind by the breath of the Divine Force, when Love flowers out from you on all creation, when Divine Knowledge floods you with a Light which illumines and transforms in a moment all that was before dark, sorrowful and obscure, when all that is becomes part of the One Reality, when the Reality is all around you, you feel at once by the spiritual contact, by the inner vision, by the illumined and seeing thought, by the vital sensation and even by the very physical sense, everywhere you see, hear, touch only the Divine. Then you can much less doubt it or deny it than you can deny or doubt daylight or air or the sun in heaven — for of these physical things you cannot

* "As men approach Me, I accept them to My love." — *Gita* 4.1 (Ed.)

be sure but they are what your senses represent them to be; but in the concrete experiences of the Divine, doubt is impossible.[51]

SRI AUROBINDO

The Supreme Presence

Sweet Mother, is there a spiritual being in everybody?

That depends on what we call "being". If for "being" we substitute "presence", yes, there is a spiritual presence in everyone. If we call "being" an organised entity, fully conscious of itself, independent, and having the power of asserting itself and ruling the rest of the nature — no! The possibility of this independent and all-powerful being is in everybody, but the realisation is the result of long efforts which sometimes extend over many lives.

In everyone, even at the very beginning, this spiritual presence, this inner light is there.... In fact, it is everywhere. I have seen it many a time in certain animals. It is like a shining point which is the basis of a certain control and protection, something which, even in half-consciousness, makes possible a certain harmony with the rest of creation so that irreparable catastrophes may not be constant and general. Without this presence the disorder created by the violences and passions of the vital would be so great that at any moment they could bring about a general catastrophe, a sort of total destruction which would prevent the progress of Nature. That presence, that spiritual light —

which could almost be called a spiritual consciousness — is within each being and all things, and because of it, in spite of all discordance, all passion, all violence, there is a minimum of general harmony which allows Nature's work to be accomplished.

And this presence becomes quite obvious in the human being, even the most rudimentary. Even in the most monstrous human being, in one who gives the impression of being an incarnation of a devil or a monster, there is something within exercising a sort of irresistible control — even in the worst, some things are impossible. And without this presence, if the being were controlled exclusively by the adverse forces, the forces of the vital, this impossibility would not exist.

Each time a wave of these monstrous adverse forces sweeps over the earth, one feels that nothing can ever stop the disorder and horror from spreading, and always, at a certain time, unexpectedly and inexplicably a control intervenes, and the wave is arrested, the catastrophe is not total. And this is because of the Presence, the supreme Presence, in matter.

But only in a few exceptional beings and after a long, very long work of preparation extending over many, many lives does this Presence change into a conscious, independent, fully organised being, all-powerful master of his dwelling-place, conscious enough, powerful enough, to be able to control not only this dwelling but what surrounds it and in a field of radiation and action that is more and more extensive... and effective.[52]

THE MOTHER

Divine Guidance behind Life

I can only state my own knowledge founded not on reasoning but on experience that there is such a guidance and that nothing is in vain in this universe.

If we look only at outward facts in their surface appearance or if we regard what we see happening around us as definitive, not as processes of a moment in a developing whole, the guidance is not apparent; at most, we may see interventions occasional or sometimes frequent. The guidance can become evident only if we go behind appearances and begin to understand the forces at work and the way of their working and their secret significance. After all, real knowledge — even scientific knowledge — comes by going behind the surface phenomena to their hidden process and causes. It is quite obvious that this world is full of suffering, and afflicted with transience to a degree that seems to justify the Gita's description of it as "this unhappy and transient world", *anityam asukham*. The question is whether it is a mere creation of Chance or governed by a mechanical inconscient Law or whether there is a meaning in it and something beyond its present appearance towards which we move. If there is a meaning and if there is something towards which things are evolving, then inevitably there must be a guidance — and that means that a supporting Consciousness and Will is there with which we can come into inner contact. If there is such a Consciousness and Will, it is not likely that it would stultify itself by annulling the world's meaning or turning it into a perpetual or eventual failure.

This world has a double aspect. It seems to be based on a material Inconscience and an ignorant mind and life full of that Inconscience: error and sorrow, death and suffering are the necessary consequence. But there is evidently too a partially successful endeavour and an imperfect growth towards Light, Knowledge, Truth, Good, Happiness, Harmony, Beauty, at least a partial flowering of these things. The meaning of this world must evidently lie in this opposition; it must be an evolution which is leading or struggling towards higher things out of a first darker appearance. Whatever guidance there is must be given under these conditions of opposition and struggle and must be leading towards that higher state of things. It is leading the individual, certainly, and the world, presumably, towards the higher state, but through the double terms of knowledge and ignorance, light and darkness, death and life, pain and pleasure, happiness and suffering; none of the terms can be excluded until the higher status is reached and established. It is not and cannot be, ordinarily, a guidance which at once rejects the darker terms, still less a guidance which brings us solely and always nothing but happiness, success and good fortune. Its main concern is with the growth of our being and consciousness, the growth towards a higher self, towards the Divine, eventually towards a higher Light, Truth and Bliss; the rest is secondary, sometimes a means, sometimes a result, not a primary purpose.

The true sense of the guidance becomes clearer when we can go deep within and see from there more intimately the play of the forces and receive intimations of the Will behind them. The surface mind can get only an imperfect glimpse. When we are in contact with the Divine or in contact with an inner knowledge and vision, we begin to see all the circumstances of our life in a new light and can observe how they all tended, without our knowing it, towards the growth of our being and consciousness, towards the work we had to do, towards some development that had to be made, — not only what seemed good, fortunate or successful but also the struggles, failures, difficulties, upheavals. But with each person the guidance works differently according to his nature, the conditions of his life, his cast of consciousness, his stage of development, his need of further experience. We are not automata but conscious beings and our mentality, our will and its decisions, our attitude to life and demand on it, our motives and movements help to determine our course: they may lead to much suffering and evil, but through it all, the guidance makes use of them for our growth in experience and consequently the development of our being and consciousness. All advance, by however devious ways, even in spite of what seems a going backwards or going astray, gathering whatever experience is necessary for the soul's destiny. When we are in close contact with the Divine, a protection can come which helps or directly guides or moves us: it does not throw aside all difficulties, sufferings or dangers, but it carries us through them and out of them — except where for a special purpose there is need of the opposite.

It is the same thing though on a larger scale and in a more complex way with the guidance of the world-movement. That seems to move according to the conditions and laws or forces of the moment through constant vicissitudes, but still there is something in it that drives towards the evolutionary purpose, although it is more difficult to see, understand and follow than in the smaller and more intimate field of the individual consciousness and life. What happens at a particular juncture of the world-action or the life of humanity, however catastrophical, is not ultimately determinative. Here, too, one has to see not only the outward play of forces in a particular case or at a particular time but also the inner and secret play, the far-off outcome, the event that lies beyond and the Will at work behind it all. Falsehood and Darkness are strong everywhere on the earth, and have always been so and at times they seem to dominate; but there have also been not only gleams but outbursts of the Light. In the mass of things and the long course of Time, whatever may be the appearance of this or that epoch or movement, the growth of Light is there and the struggle towards better things does not cease. At the present time Falsehood and Darkness have gathered their forces and are extremely powerful; but even if we reject the assertion of the mystics and prophets since early times that such a condition of things must precede the Manifestation and is even a sign of its approach, yet it does not necessarily indicate the decisive victory even temporary — of the Falsehood. It merely means that the struggle between the Forces is at its acme. The result may very well be the stronger emergence of the best that can be: for the world-movement often works in that way.[53]

SRI AUROBINDO

Interpreting the Guidance

The difficulties and obstacles met on the path when one wants to attain a certain aim — are they sometimes a sign that this decision, this plan or project was faulty from the beginning and that hence one

> *should not persist or, on the contrary, do these difficulties indicate a victory to be won, a transformation to be attained? Are they a sign that one must persevere and hold fast? I am not speaking here of the decision to follow the path of Yoga, but of the little things connected with work, sports or other activities. In other words, how to recognise and interpret the Guidance which comes through circumstances or relations with others and through experience?*

I believe this is only an apparent contradiction.

If one wants to follow a discipline of yoga, naturally, before undertaking anything one must try to discern and know if the inspiration received is a real one, coming from the Divine, or whether it is simply a reaction to outer circumstances and an impulse, either vital or mental. It is quite important, even very important, to try to discern and act in full knowledge of the cause. But there are very many things one does and about which one is not in the habit of thinking beforehand. When the circumstance comes, one obeys it, so to say. And, indeed, these things, like almost everything one does in life, are not important in themselves. The only thing that matters is the *attitude* with which they are done. The fact that you do something because that action is present there before you for one reason or another and that you are, so to say, always obliged to act as long as you are in the outer life — all this has a certain importance from the point of view of the management of life if these acts are liable to have far-reaching consequences in life, as for example, getting married or going to live in one place or another or taking up one occupation or another; these things are generally considered important, and they are so to a certain extent; but even for them, from the point of view of yoga, everything depends much more on the attitude one takes than on the thing itself. And so, above all, for all the very small actions of daily life, the importance is reduced to a minimum.

There are some scrupulous people who set problems to themselves and find it very difficult to solve them, because they state the problem wrongly. I knew a young woman who was a theosophist and was trying to practise; she told me, "We are taught that the divine Will must prevail in all that we do, but in the morning when I have my breakfast, how can I know whether God wants me to put two lumps of sugar in my coffee or only one?"... And it was quite touching, you know, and I had some trouble explaining to her that the spirit in which she drank her coffee, the attitude she had towards her food, was much more important than the number of lumps of sugar she put into it.*

It is the same with all the little things one does at every moment. The divine Consciousness does not work in the human way, It does not decide how many lumps of sugar you will put in your coffee. It gradually puts you in the right attitude towards actions, things — an attitude of consecration, suppleness, assent, aspiration, goodwill, plasticity, effort for progress — and this is what counts, much more than the small decision you take at every second. One may try to find out what is the truest thing to do, but it is not by a mental discussion or a mental problem that these

* About this story, a disciple remembers Mother telling him something to this effect: "Now I would no longer laugh at this poor lady. I am not sure that the Lord does not also attend to the number of lumps of sugar we put in our coffee!"

things can be resolved. It is in fact by an inner attitude which *creates* an atmosphere of harmony — progressive harmony — in which all one does will necessarily be the best thing that could be done in those particular circumstances. And the ideal would be an attitude complete enough for the action to be spontaneous, dictated by something other than an outer reason. But that is an ideal — for which one must aspire and which one can realise after some time. Till then, to take care always to keep the true attitude, the true aspiration, is much more important than to decide whether one will do gymnastic-marching or not and whether one will go to a certain class or not. Because these things have no real importance in themselves, they have only an altogether relative importance, the only important thing is just to keep the true orientation in one's aspiration and a living will for progress.

As a general rule, and so that the experience may have its full benefit, when one has undertaken something one must do it with persistence, without caring for obstacles and difficulties, until an absolutely irrefutable event indicates that one no longer has to do it. This happens very rarely. Usually, things follow their own curve and when they reach an issue — either they have come to an end or have produced the desired result — one becomes aware of the reason for doing them. But the obstacles, oppositions — or encouragements — should not be considered as irrefutable signs to be followed, for these things may have very different meanings according to the case, and it is not at all on the basis of these outer events that one must judge the validity of one's undertaking.

When one is very attentive and very sincere, one can have an indication, an inner but perceptible indication, of the value of what one has undertaken or the action one is doing. Truly, for someone who has an entire goodwill, that is, who in all sincerity, with the whole conscious part of his being, wants to do the right thing in the right way, there is always an indication; if for some reason or other one launches upon a more or less fatal action, one *always* feels an uneasiness in the region of the solar plexus; an uneasiness which is not violent, which doesn't compel recognition dramatically, but is very perceptible to someone who is attentive — something like a sort of regret, like a lack of assent. It may go as far as a kind of refusal to collaborate. But I must stress it, without violence, without brutal self-assertion: it makes no noise, does not hurt, it is at the most a slight uneasiness. And if you disregard it, if you pay no attention, attach no importance to it, after a little while it will completely disappear and there will be nothing any longer.

It is not that it increases with the growing error, on the contrary, it disappears and the consciousness becomes veiled.

Therefore, one cannot give this as a sure sign, for if you have disobeyed this little indication several times, well, it will no longer come. But I tell you that if in all sincerity you are very attentive to it, then it will be a very sure and precious guide.

But if there is an uneasiness, it comes at the beginning, almost immediately, and when it doesn't show itself, well, no matter what one has started, it is preferable to do it to the very end so that the experience may be complete, unless one receives, as I said, an absolutely precise and categorical indication that it should not be done.[54]

THE MOTHER

The Divine Power behind Personal Effort

Always indeed it is the higher Power that acts. Our sense of personal effort and aspiration comes from the attempt of the egoistic mind to identify itself in a wrong and imperfect way with the workings of the divine Force. It persists in applying to experience on a supernormal plane the ordinary terms of mentality which it applies to its normal experiences in the world. In the world we act with the sense of egoism; we claim the universal forces that work in us as our own; we claim as the effect of our personal will, wisdom, force, virtue the selective, formative, progressive action of the Transcendent in this frame of mind, life and body. Enlightenment brings to us the knowledge that the ego is only an instrument; we begin to perceive and feel that these things are our own in the sense that they belong to our supreme and integral Self, one with the Transcendent, not to the instrumental ego. Our limitations and distortions are our contribution to the working; the true power in it is the Divine's. When the human ego realises that its will is a tool, its wisdom ignorance and childishness, its power an infant's groping, its virtue a pretentious impurity, and learns to trust itself to that which transcends it, that is its salvation. The apparent freedom and self-assertion of our personal being to which we are so profoundly attached, conceal a most pitiable subjection to a thousand suggestions, impulsions, forces which we have made extraneous to our little person. Our ego, boasting of freedom, is at every moment the slave, toy and puppet of countless beings, powers, forces, influences in universal Nature. The self-abnegation of the ego in the Divine is its self-fulfilment; its surrender to that which transcends it is its liberation from bonds and limits and its perfect freedom.[55]

SRI AUROBINDO

Asking from the Divine

If, for example, one wants to know something or one needs guidance, or something else, how can one have it from the Divine, according to one's need?

By asking the Divine for it. If you do not ask Him, how can you have it?

If you turn to the Divine and have full trust and ask Him, you will get what you need — not necessarily what you imagine you need; but the true thing you need, you will get. But you must ask Him for it.

You must make the experiment sincerely; you must not endeavour to get it by all sorts of external means and then expect the Divine to give it to you, without even having asked Him. Indeed, when you want somebody to give you something, you ask him for it, don't you? And why do you expect the Divine to give it to you without your having asked Him for it?

In the ordinary consciousness the movement is just the opposite. You assume something, saying, "I need this, I need this relationship, I need this affection, I need this knowledge, etc. Well, the Divine ought to give it to me, otherwise He is not the Divine." That is to say, you reverse the problem completely.

First of all, you say, "I need." Do you know whether

you truly need it or whether it is only an impression you have or a desire or quite an ignorant movement? First point: you know nothing about it.

Second point: it is precisely your own will you want to impose upon the Divine, telling Him, "I need this." And then you don't even ask Him for it: "Give it to me." You say, "I need it. Therefore, since I need it, it must come to me, quite naturally, spontaneously; it's the Divine's job to give me all that I need."

But if it so happens that truly you don't know what you need and it is merely an illusion and not a truth and that, into the bargain, you ask it from life around you and don't turn to the Divine, don't create any relationship between yourself and Him, don't think of Him or turn to Him with at least some sincerity in your attitude, then, as you ask nothing from Him, there is no reason for Him to give you anything.

But if you ask Him, as He is the Divine He knows a little better than you what you need; He will give you what you need.

Or else, if you insist and want to impose your own will, He may give you what you want in order to enlighten you and make you conscious of your mistake, that it was truly not the thing you needed. And then you begin to protest — I don't mean you personally, I am speaking of all human beings — and you say, "Why has the Divine given me something which harms me?" — completely forgetting that it was you who asked for it!

In both cases you protest all the same. If He gives you what you ask and then that brings you more harm than good, you protest. And again, if He doesn't give it, you also protest: "What! I told Him I needed it and He doesn't give it to me."

In both cases you protest, and the poor Divine is accused.

Only, if instead of all that, you simply have an aspiration within you, an urge, an intense ardent need to find That, which you conceive more or less clearly to be the Truth of your being, the Source of all things, the supreme Good, the Answer to all we desire, the Solution to all problems; if there is this intense need in you and you aspire to realise it, you won't any longer say to the Divine, "Give me this, give me that", or, "I need this, I must have that." You will tell Him, "Do what is necessary for me and lead me to the Truth of my being. Give me what Thou in Thy supreme Wisdom seest as the thing I need."

And then you are sure of not being mistaken, and He will not give you something which harms you.

There is a still higher step, but it's a little more difficult to begin with that.

But the first one is already a much truer approach than that of telling the Divine, "I need this. Give it to me." For indeed, very few people really know what they need — very few. And the proof of it is that they are always in pursuit of the fulfilment of their desires, all their effort is bent upon that, and each time one of their desires is fulfilled, they are disappointed. And they pass on to another.

And after much seeking, making many mistakes, suffering a good deal and being very disappointed, then, sometimes, one begins to grow wise and wonders if there isn't a way out of all this, that is to say, a way to come out of one's own ignorance.

And it is then, at that moment that one can do this (*Mother opens her arms*): "Here I am, take me and lead me along the true path."

Then all begins to go well.[56]

THE MOTHER

Allowing the Lord to Do It

You are faced with a so-called problem: what should you say, what should you do, how should you act? There is nothing to do, nothing, you only have to say to the Lord, "There, You see, it is like that" — that's all. And then you stay very quiet. And then quite spontaneously, without thinking about it, without reflection, without calculation, nothing, nothing, without the slightest effort — you do what has to be done. That is to say, the Lord does it, it is no longer you. He does it, He arranges the circumstances, He arranges the people, He puts the words into your mouth or your pen — He does everything, everything, everything, everything; you have nothing more to do but to allow yourself to live blissfully.

I am more and more convinced that people do not really want it.

But clearing the ground is difficult, the work of clearing the ground beforehand.

But you don't even need to do it! He does it for you.

But they are constantly breaking in: the old consciousness, the old thoughts....

Yes, they try to come in again, by habit. You only have

to say, "Lord, You see, You see, You see, it is like that" — that's all. "Lord, You see, You see this, You see that, You see this fool" — and it is all over immediately. And it changes automatically, my child, without the slightest effort. Simply to be sincere, that is to say, to *truly* want everything to be right. You are perfectly conscious that you can do nothing about it, that you have no capacity. I feel more and more that this amalgam of matter, like this, of cells, all that, is pitiful. It is pitiful! I do not know whether there are certain states in which people feel powerful, wonderful, luminous, capable; but for me it is because they do not really know what they are like! When you really see how you are made — it is really nothing, nothing. But it is capable of everything, provided... provided that you allow the Lord to act. But there is always something that wants to do it by itself; that's the trouble, otherwise...

No, you may be full of an excellent goodwill and then *you want* to do it. That's what complicates everything. Or else you don't have faith, you believe that the Lord will not be able to do it and that you must do it yourself, because He does not know! (*Mother laughs.*) This, this kind of stupidity is very common. "How can He see things? We live in a world of Falsehood, how can He see Falsehood and see..." But He sees the thing as it is! Exactly!

I am not speaking of people of no intelligence, I am speaking of people who are intelligent and who try — there is a kind of conviction, like that, somewhere, even in people who know that we live in a world of Ignorance and Falsehood and that there is a Lord who is All-Truth. They say, "Precisely because He is All-Truth, He does not understand. (*Mother laughs.*) He does not understand our falsehood, I must deal with it myself." That is very strong, very common. Ah! we make complications for nothing.[57]

THE MOTHER

Pressure of the Spirit

> The mental intelligence and its main power of reason cannot change the principle and persistent character of human life, it can only effect various mechanisations, manipulations, developments and formulations. But neither is mind as a whole, even spiritualised, able to change it; spirituality liberates and illumines the inner being, it helps mind to communicate with what is higher than itself, to escape even from itself.... —*Sri Aurobindo*

Sweet Mother, what is the meaning of "spirituality... helps mind... to escape from itself"?

As long as the mind is convinced that it is the summit of human consciousness, that there is nothing beyond and above it, it takes its own functioning to be a perfect one and is fully satisfied with the progress it can make within the limits of this functioning, and with an increase of clarity, precision, complexity, suppleness, plasticity in its movements.

It always has a spontaneous tendency to feel very satisfied with itself and with what it can do, and if there were no greater force than its own, a higher power which irrefutably shows it its own limitations, its poverty, it would never make any effort to find its way out of all that by the right door: liberation into a higher and truer mode of being.

When the spiritual force is able to act, when it begins to have an influence, it jolts the mind's self-satisfaction and, by continuous pressure, begins to make it feel that beyond it there is something higher and truer; then a little of its characteristic vanity gives way under this influence and as soon as it realises that it is limited, ignorant, incapable of reaching the true truth, liberation begins with the possibility of opening to something beyond. But it must *feel* the power, the beauty, the force of this beyond to be able to surrender. It must be able to perceive its incapacity and its limitations in the presence of something higher than itself, otherwise how could it ever feel its own weakness!

Sometimes one single contact is enough, something that makes a little rent in that self-satisfaction; then the yearning to go beyond, the need for a purer light awaken, and with this awakening comes the aspiration to win them, and with the aspiration liberation begins, and one day, breaking all limits, one blossoms in the infinite Light.

If there were not this constant Pressure, simultaneously from within and without, from above and from the profoundest depths, nothing would ever change.

Even with that, how much time is required for things to change! What obstinate resistance in this lower nature, what blind and stupid attachment to the animal ways of the being, what a refusal to liberate oneself!

(*Silence*)

In the whole manifestation there is an infinite Grace constantly at work to bring the world out of the misery, the obscurity and the stupidity in which it lies. From all time this Grace has been at work, unremitting in its effort, and how many thousands of years were necessary for this world to awaken to the need for something greater, more true, more beautiful.

Everyone can gauge, from the resistance he meets in his own being, the tremendous resistance which the world opposes to the work of the Grace.

And it is only when one understands that *all* external things, all mental constructions, all material efforts are vain, futile, if they are not entirely consecrated to this Light and Force from above, to this Truth which is trying to express itself, that one is ready to make decisive progress. So the only truly effective attitude is a perfect, total, fervent giving of our being to That which is above us and which alone has the power to change everything.

When you open to the Spirit within you it brings you a first foretaste of that higher life which alone is worth living, then comes the will to rise to that, the hope of reaching it, the certitude that this is possible, and finally the strength to make the necessary effort and the resolution to go to the very end.

First one must wake up, then one can conquer.[58]

THE MOTHER

State of Receptivity

There are many different reasons which make one feel at times more alive, more full of force and joy.... Usually, in ordinary life, there are people who, due to their very constitution, the way they are made, are in a certain harmony with

Nature, as though they breathed with the same rhythm, and these people are usually always joyful, happy; they succeed in all they do, they avoid many troubles and catastrophes, indeed they are in harmony with the rhythm of life and Nature. And, moreover, there are days when one is in contact with the divine Consciousness which is at work, with the Grace, and then everything is tinged, coloured with this Presence, and things which usually seem to you dull and uninteresting become charming, pleasant, attractive, instructive — everything lives and vibrates, and is full of promise and force. So, when one opens to that, one feels stronger, freer, happier, full of energy, and *everything* has a meaning. One understands why things are as they are and one participates in the general movement.

There are other times when, for some reason or other, one is clouded or closed or down in a hole, and so one no longer feels anything and all things lose their taste, their interest, their value; one goes about like a walking block of wood.

Now, if one is able to consciously unite with one's psychic being, one can *always* be in this state of receptivity, inner joy, energy, progress, communion with the divine Presence. And when one is in communion with That, one sees it everywhere, in everything, and all things take on their true meaning.

On what does that depend?... On an inner rhythm. Perhaps a grace. In any case on a receptivity to something that is beyond you.[59]

THE MOTHER

The Divine Gives Himself

Sweet Mother, what is meant by "the Divine gives Himself"?

It means exactly this: that the more you give yourself the more you have the experience — it is not just a feeling or impression or sensation, it is a total experience — that the more you give yourself to the Divine the more He is with you, totally, constantly, at every minute, in all your thoughts, all your needs, and that there's no aspiration which does not receive an immediate answer; and you have the sense of a complete, constant intimacy, of a total nearness. It is as though you carried... as though the Divine were all the time with you; you walk and He walks with you, you sleep and He sleeps with you, you eat and He eats with you, you think and He thinks with you, you love and He is the love you have. But for this one must give himself entirely, totally, exclusively, reserve nothing, keep nothing for himself and not keep back anything, not disperse anything also: the least little thing in your being which is not given to the Divine is a waste; it is the wasting of your joy, something that lessens your happiness by that much, and all that you don't give to the Divine is as though you were holding it in the way of the possibility of the Divine's giving Himself to you. You don't feel Him close to yourself, constantly with you, because you don't belong to Him, because you belong to hundreds of other things and people; in your thought, your action, your feelings, impulses... there are millions of things which you do not give Him, and that is why you don't feel Him always with you, because all these things are so many screens and walls between Him and you. But if you give Him everything, if you keep back nothing, He will be constantly and totally with you in all that you do, in all that you think, all that you feel, always, at each moment. But for this you must give yourself absolutely, keep back nothing; each little thing that you hold back is a stone you put down to build up a wall between the Divine and yourself. And then later you complain: "Oh, I don't feel Him!"[60]

THE MOTHER

The Law of Sacrifice

The law of sacrifice is the common divine action that was thrown out into the world in its beginning as a symbol of the solidarity of the universe. It is by the attraction of this law that a divinising, a saving power descends to limit and correct and gradually to eliminate the errors of an egoistic and self-divided creation. This descent, this sacrifice of the Purusha, the Divine Soul submitting itself to Force and Matter so that it may inform and illuminate them, is the seed of redemption of this world of Inconscience and Ignorance. For 'with sacrifice as their companion,' says the Gita, 'the All-Father created these peoples.' The acceptance of the law of sacrifice is a practical recognition by the ego that it is neither alone in the world nor chief in the world. It is its admission that, even in this much fragmented existence, there is beyond itself and behind that which is not its own egoistic person, something greater and completer, a diviner All which demands from it subordination and service.

Sri Aurobindo

Sweet Mother, what does the "sacrifice to the Divine" mean?

It is self-giving. It is the word the Gita uses for self-giving.

Only, the sacrifice is mutual, this is what Sri Aurobindo says at the beginning: the Divine has sacrificed Himself in Matter to awaken consciousness in Matter, which had become inconscient. And it is this sacrifice, this giving of the Divine in Matter, that is to say, His dispersion in Matter, which justifies the sacrifice of Matter to the Divine and makes it obligatory; for it is one and the same reciprocal movement. It is because the Divine has given Himself in Matter and scattered Himself everywhere in Matter to awaken it to the divine consciousness, that Matter is automatically under the obligation to give itself to the Divine. It is a mutual and reciprocal sacrifice.

And this is the great secret of the Gita: the affirmation of the divine Presence in the very heart of Matter. And that is why, Matter must sacrifice itself to the Divine, automatically, even unconsciously—whether one wants it or not, this is what happens.

Only, when it is done unconsciously, one doesn't have the joy of sacrifice; while if it is done consciously, one has the joy of sacrifice which is the supreme joy.

The word "sacrifice" in French has slightly too narrow a sense, which it doesn't have in the original Sanskrit; for in French sacrifice implies a sort of suffering, almost a regret. While in Sanskrit this sense is not there at all; it corresponds to "self-giving"... .

But how can a sacrifice be made when one is unconscious?

It is made automatically.

Whether you know it or not, whether you want it or not, you are all united by the divine Presence which, though it appears fragmented, is yet One. The Divine is One, He only appears fragmented in things and beings. And because this Unity is a fact, whether you are aware of it or not doesn't alter the fact at all. And whether you want it or not, you are in spite of everything subject to this Unity.

This is what I have explained to you I don't know how many times: you think you are separate from one another, but it is the same single Substance which is in you all, despite differences in appearance; and a vibration in one centre automatically awakens a vibration in another.

So, no effort is to be made to improve the sacrifice, there is no need to make an effort?

I don't understand this conclusion at all.

If you are happy to be unhappy, that's all right, it is your own affair; if you are content to be unhappy and to suffer and remain in the ignorance and inconscience you are in, stay there. But if this does not satisfy you, if you want to be conscious and you want suffering to cease, then you must make constant efforts to become conscious of the sacrifice and to make your sacrifice consciously instead of unconsciously.

Everything turns around the consciousness, the fact of being or not being conscious. And it is only in the supreme Consciousness that you can attain the perfect expression of yourself.

But that the Oneness exists, even if you feel just the opposite, is a fact you can do nothing about, for it is a divine action and a divine fact — it is a divine action and a divine fact. If you are conscious of the Divine, you become conscious of this fact. If you are not conscious of the Divine, the fact exists but you simply are not conscious of it — that's all.

So, everything turns around a phenomenon of consciousness. And the world is in a state of obscurity, suffering, misery, of... everything, all it is, simply because it is not conscious of the Divine, because it has cut off the connection in its consciousness, because its consciousness is separated from the Divine. That is to say, it has become unconscious.

For the true consciousness is the divine Consciousness. If you cut yourself off from the divine Consciousness, you become absolutely unconscious; that is exactly what has happened. And so, everything there is, the world as it is, your consciousness as it is, things in the state they are in, are the result of this separation of the consciousness and its immediate obscuration.

The minute the individual consciousness is separated from the divine Consciousness, it enters what we call the inconscience, and it is this inconscience that is the cause of all its miseries.

But all that is, is essentially divine, and the divine Oneness is a fact, you can't do anything about it; all your unconsciousness and all your denials will change nothing — it is a fact, it's like that.

And the conclusion is this, that the true transformation is the transformation of consciousness — all the rest will follow automatically.

Does the inconscient aspire to become conscious?

No. It is the Divine in the inconscient who aspires for the Divine in the consciousness. That is to say, without the Divine there would be no aspiration; without the consciousness hidden in the inconscient, there would be no possibility of changing the inconscience to consciousness. But because at the very heart of the inconscient there is the divine Consciousness, you aspire, and necessarily — this is what he says — automatically, mechanically, the sacrifice is made. And this is why when one says, "It is not *you* who aspire, it is the Divine, it is not *you* who make progress, it is the Divine, it is not *you* who are conscious, it is the Divine" — these are not mere words, it is a fact. And it is simply your ignorance and your unconsciousness which prevent you from realising it.[61]

THE MOTHER

The Lord is not Far Away

There is something I have often wondered about: when one prays to the Lord, when one wants to make Him understand that something is wrong, I always have the impression that one must concentrate very hard and that after all one is calling to something far away. Is that right? Or is it really...

That depends on us!

Now I can feel Him everywhere, all the time, all the time... even a physical contact — it is subtle physical, but physical — in things, in the air, in people, in... like this.

(*Mother presses her hands to her face.*) And then, it is not far to go, all I have to do is this (*Mother turns her hands slightly inwards*), one second of concentration — He is there! He is there, He is everywhere. He is far away only when we think He is far away.

Naturally, when we begin to think of all the zones, all the planes of universal consciousness and that it is at the very end, at the very end, right at the very end, then it becomes very far away, very, very far! (*Mother laughs.*) But when we think that He is everywhere, that He is everything and that it is only our perception that prevents us from seeing Him and feeling Him and that we only have to do this (*Mother turns her hands inwards*); it is a movement like this and like that (*Mother turns her hands alternately inwards and outwards*), it becomes very concrete: you do this (*outward movement*), everything becomes artificial, hard, dry, false, untrue, artificial; you do this (*inward movement*), everything becomes wide, tranquil, luminous, peaceful, vast, joyful. And it is simply this, that (*Mother turns her hands alternately inwards and outwards*). How? Where? It cannot be described, it is only, *only* a movement of consciousness, nothing else. A movement of consciousness. And the difference between the true consciousness and the false consciousness becomes more and more precise, and at the same time, *thin* — you don't have to do "great things" to come out of it. Before that, one has the impression that one is living inside something and that a great interiorisation, concentration, absorption, is needed to get out of it; but now the impression is of something one accepts (*Mother screens her face with her hand*), something like a thin little peel that is very hard — very hard but malleable, very, very dry, very thin, very thin, something like putting on a mask; and then one does this (*gesture*), and it disappears.

One can foresee the time when it will not be necessary to be aware of the mask; it will be so thin that one will be able to see, to feel, to act through it with no need to put the mask on again. That is what has just begun.

But this Presence in all things.... It is a vibration, but it is a vibration that contains everything — a vibration which contains a kind of infinite power, infinite delight and infinite peace, of vastness, vastness, vastness; there are no limits.... But it is only a vibration, it does not... Oh, Lord! it cannot be thought, so it cannot be said. If you think, as soon as you think, the whole muddle begins again. That is why one cannot speak.

No, He is very far away because you think He is very far away. Even, you know, if you think He is there, like this (*gesture close to her face*) touching you... if you could feel — it is not like the touch of a person, it is not like that. It is not something alien, external, which comes in from outside. It is not that.... It is everywhere.

Then you feel — everywhere, everywhere, everywhere: inside, outside, everywhere, everywhere — Him, nothing but Him — Him, His vibration.[62]

THE MOTHER

Gratitude Must Come With Devotion

... devotion is all very well, but unless it is accompanied by many other things it too may make many mistakes. It may meet with great difficulties.

You have devotion, and you keep your ego. And then your ego makes you do all sorts of things out of devotion, things which are terribly egoistic. That is to say, you think only of yourself, not of others, nor of the world, nor of the work, nor of what ought to be done — you think only of your devotion. And you become tremendously egoistic. And so, when you find out that the Divine, for some reason, does not answer to your devotion with the enthusiasm you expected of Him, you despair and fall back into the same three difficulties I was just speaking about: either the Divine is cruel — we have read that, there are many such stories, of enthusiastic devotees who abuse the Divine because He is no longer as gentle and near to them as before, He has withdrawn, "Why hast Thou deserted me? Thou hast abandoned me, O monster!..." They don't dare to say this, but think it, or else they say, "Oh! I must have made such a serious mistake that I am thrown out", and they fall into despair.

But there is another movement which should constantly accompany devotion.... That kind of sense of gratitude that the Divine exists; that feeling of a marvelling thankfulness which truly fills you with a sublime joy at the fact that the Divine exists, that there is something in the universe which is the Divine, that it is not just the monstrosity we see, that there is the Divine, the Divine exists. And each time that the least thing puts you either directly or indirectly in contact with this sublime Reality of divine existence, the heart is filled with so intense, so marvellous a joy, such a gratitude as of all things has the most delightful taste.

There is nothing which gives you a joy equal to that of gratitude. One hears a bird sing, sees a lovely flower, looks at a little child, observes an act of generosity, reads a beautiful sentence, looks at the setting sun, no matter what, suddenly this comes upon you, this kind of emotion — indeed so deep, so intense — that the world manifests the Divine, that there is something behind the world which is the Divine.

So I find that devotion without gratitude is quite incomplete, gratitude must come with devotion.[63]

THE MOTHER

Laughing With the Lord

God's laughter is sometimes very coarse and unfit for polite ears; He is not satisfied with being Molière, He must needs also be Aristophanes and Rabelais.

If men took life less seriously, they could very soon make it more perfect. God never takes His works seriously; therefore one looks out on this wonderful Universe.

Shame has admirable results and both in aesthetics and in morality we could ill spare it; but for all that it is a badge of weakness and the proof of ignorance.

Sri Aurobindo

One might ask how taking things seriously has prevented life from being more perfect.

Virtue has always spent its time eliminating whatever it found bad in life, and if all the virtues of the various countries of the world had been put together, very few things would remain in existence.

Virtue claims to seek perfection, but perfection is a totality. So the two movements contradict each other. A virtue that eliminates, reduces, fixes limits, and a perfection that accepts everything, rejects nothing but puts each thing in its place, obviously cannot agree.

Taking life seriously generally consists of two movements: the first one is to give importance to things that probably have none, and the second is to want life to be reduced to a certain number of qualities that are considered pure and worthy of existence. In some people—for example, those Sri Aurobindo speaks about here, the "polite" or the puritans—this virtue becomes dry, arid, grey, aggressive and it finds fault everywhere, in everything that is joyful and free and happy.

The only way to make life perfect—I mean here, life on earth, of course—is to look at it from high enough to see it as a whole, not only in its present totality, but in the whole of the past, present and future: what it has been, what it is and what it will be—one must be able to see everything at once. Because that is the only way to put everything in its place. Nothing can be eliminated, nothing *should* be eliminated, but each thing must be in its place in total harmony with all the rest. And then all these things that seem so "bad", so "reprehensible", so "unacceptable" to the puritan mind, would become movements of delight and freedom in a totally divine life. And then nothing would prevent us from knowing, understanding, feeling and living this wonderful laughter of the Supreme who takes infinite delight in watching Himself live infinitely.

This delight, this wonderful laughter that dissolves every shadow, every pain, every suffering! You only have to go deep enough within yourself to find the inner Sun, to let yourself be flooded by it; and then there is nothing but a cascade of harmonious, luminous, sunlit laughter, which leaves no room for any shadow or pain.

In fact, even the greatest difficulties, even the greatest sorrows, even the greatest physical pain — if you can look at them from that standpoint, from there, you see the unreality of the difficulty, the unreality of the sorrow, the unreality of the pain — and there is nothing but a joyful and luminous vibration.

In fact, this is the most powerful way of dissolving difficulties, overcoming sorrows and removing pain. The first two are relatively easy — I say relatively — the last one is more difficult because we are in the habit of considering the body and its feelings to be extremely concrete, positive; but it is the same thing, it is simply because we have not learnt, we are not in the habit of regarding our body as something fluid, plastic, uncertain, malleable. We have not learnt to bring into it this luminous laughter that dissolves all darkness, all difficulty, all discord, all disharmony, everything that jars, that weeps and wails.

And this Sun, this Sun of divine laughter is at the centre of all things, the truth of all things: we must learn to see it, to feel it, to live it.

And for that, let us avoid people who take life seriously; they are very boring people.

As soon as the atmosphere becomes grave you can be sure that something is wrong, that there is a troubling influence, an old habit trying to reassert itself, which should not be accepted. All this regret, all this remorse, the feeling of being unworthy, of being at fault — and then one step further and you have the sense of sin. Oh! To me it all seems to belong to another age, an age of darkness.

But everything that persists, that tries to cling and endure, all these prohibitions and this habit of cutting life in two — into small things and big things, the sacred and the profane.... "What!" say the people who profess to follow a spiritual life, "how can you make such little things, such insignificant things the object of spiritual experience?" And yet this is an experience that becomes more and more concrete and real, even materially; it's not that there are "some things" where the Lord is and "some things" where He is not. The Lord is *always* there. He takes nothing seriously, everything amuses Him and He plays with you, if you know how to play. You do not know how to play, people do not know how to play. But how well He knows how to play! How well He plays! With everything, with the smallest things: you have some things to put on the table? Don't feel that you have to think and arrange, no, let's play: let's put this one here and that one there, and this one like that. And then another time it's different again.... What a good game and such fun!

So, it is agreed, we shall try to learn how to laugh with the Lord.[64]

THE MOTHER

The Action of Divine Grace

I have said somewhere, or maybe written, that no matter how great your faith and trust in the divine Grace, no matter how great your capacity to see it at work in all circumstances, at every moment, at every point in life, you will never succeed in understanding the marvellous immensity of Its Action, and the precision, the exactitude with which this Action is accomplished; you will never be able to grasp to what extent the Grace does everything, is behind everything, organises everything, conducts everything, so that the march forward to the divine realisation may be as swift, as complete, as total and harmonious as possible, considering the circumstances of the world.

As soon as you are in contact with It, there is not a second in time, not a point in space, which does not show you *dazzlingly* this perpetual work of the Grace, this constant intervention of the Grace.

And once you have seen this, you feel you are never equal to it, for you should never forget it, never have any fears, any anguish, any regrets, any recoils... or even suffering. If one were in union with this Grace, if one saw It everywhere, one would begin living a life of exultation, of all-power, of infinite happiness.

And that would be the best possible collaboration in the divine Work.[65]

THE MOTHER

Experiencing All Relationships in the Divine

> ... he [the seeker of the integral yoga] has felt a Divinity who is all these things, a Bringer of Light, a Guide and All-Knower, a Master of Force, a Giver of Bliss, Friend, Helper, Father, Mother, Playmate in the world-game, an

absolute Master of his being, his soul's Beloved and Lover. — *Sri Aurobindo*

Can the Godhead be all these things at once for anybody?

Yes, and many more.

This is only a very brief description!

But here too, if one wants to have this experience, one must not seek in life and among men for these relationships, because if one seeks them in the ordinary life, as ordinary relationships, one becomes incapable of feeling them exactly as the Divine can give them. And usually, most people, even those who have a living soul, seek these relations with the Divine only after they have had the most bitter and disappointing experiences in their search for human relationships.

This makes them lose much time and wastes a lot of energy. And usually, they are already quite worn out and spent when they reach the state in which they are capable of having these relations in all their splendour with the divine Presence.

That means much time lost and much wastage of energy; but it would seem that very few people can go straight avoiding all these roundabout ways. Mostly, when they are told that there is a divine Joy and a divine Plenitude which far surpass all they can imagine in ordinary life, they don't believe it; and to believe it they must have, as I said, gone through a painful experience of all that is false, deceptive and disappointing in ordinary relationships.

It is said that example is the best teacher, but in fact

there are very few who care to follow an example — especially when the examples are a little too far beyond them. They all want to have their own experience; they have the right to it, but that makes the path interminable.[66]

THE MOTHER

Discovering Divine Love

It is said that to become conscious of divine Love all other love has to be abandoned. What is the best way of rejecting the other love which clings so obstinately (laughter) *and does not easily leave us?*

To go through it. Ah!

To go through, to see what is behind it, not to stop at the appearance, not to be satisfied with the outer form, to look for the principle which is behind this love, and not be content until one has found the *origin* of the feeling in oneself. Then the outer form will crumble of itself and you will be in contact with the divine Love which is behind all things.

That is the best way.

To want to get rid of the one in order to find the other is very difficult. It is almost impossible. For human nature is so limited, so full of contradictions and so exclusive in its movements that if one wants to reject love in its lower form, that is to say, human love as human beings experience it, if one makes an inner effort to reject it, one usually rejects the entire capacity of feeling love and becomes like a stone. And then sometimes one has to wait for years or centuries before there is a reawakening in oneself of the capacity to receive and manifest love.

Therefore, the best way when love comes, in whatever form it may be, is to try and pierce through its outer appearance and find the divine principle which is behind and which gives it existence. Naturally, it is full of snares and difficulties, but it is more effective. That is to say, instead of ceasing to love because one loves wrongly, one must cease to love wrongly and want to love well.

For instance, love between human beings, in all its forms, the love of parents for children, of children for parents, of brothers and sisters, of friends and lovers, is all tainted with ignorance, selfishness and all the other defects which are man's ordinary drawbacks; so instead of completely ceasing to love — which, besides, is very difficult as Sri Aurobindo says, which would simply dry up the heart and serve no end — one must learn how to love better: to love with devotion, with self-giving, self-abnegation, and to struggle, not against love itself, but against its distorted forms: against all forms of monopolising, of attachment, possessiveness, jealousy, and all the feelings which accompany these main movements. Not to want to possess, to dominate; and not to want to impose one's will, one's whims, one's desires; not to want to take, to receive, but to give; not to insist on the other's response, but be content with one's own love; not to seek one's personal interest and joy and the fulfilment of one's personal desire, but to be satisfied with the giving of one's love and affection; and not to ask for any response. Simply to be happy to love, nothing more.

If you do that, you have taken a great stride forward

and can, through this attitude, gradually advance farther in the feeling itself, and realise one day that love is not something personal, that love is a universal divine feeling which manifests through you more or less finely, but which in its essence is something divine.

The first step is to stop being selfish. For everyone it is the same thing, not only for those who want to do yoga but also in ordinary life: if one wants to know how to love, one must not love oneself first and above all selfishly; one must give oneself to the object of love without exacting anything in return. This discipline is elementary in order to surmount oneself and lead a life which is not altogether gross.

As for yoga we may add something else: it is as I said in the beginning, the will to pierce through this limited and human form of love and discover the principle of divine Love which is behind it. Then one is sure to get a result. This is better than drying up one's heart. It is perhaps a little more difficult but it is better in every way, for like this, instead of egoistically making others suffer, well, one may leave them quiet in their own movement and only make an effort to transform oneself without imposing one's will on others, which even in ordinary life is a step towards something higher and a little more harmonious.[67]

THE MOTHER

The Hour of God

There are moments when the Spirit moves among men and the breath of the Lord is abroad upon the waters of our being; there are others when it retires and men are left to act in the strength or the weakness of their own egoism. The first are periods when even a little effort produces great results and changes destiny; the second are spaces of time when much labour goes to the making of a little result. It is true that the latter may prepare the former, may be the little smoke of sacrifice going up to heaven which calls down the rain of God's bounty. Unhappy is the man or the nation which, when the divine moment arrives, is found sleeping or unprepared to use it, because the lamp has not been kept trimmed for the welcome and the ears are sealed to the call. But thrice woe to them who are strong and ready, yet waste the force or misuse the moment; for them is irreparable loss or a great destruction. In the hour of God cleanse thy soul of all self-deceit and hypocrisy and vain self-flattering that thou mayst look straight into thy spirit and hear that which summons it. All insincerity of nature, once thy defence against the eye of the Master and the light of the ideal, becomes now a gap in thy armour and invites the blow. Even if thou conquer for the moment, it is the worse for thee, for the blow shall come afterwards and cast thee down in the midst of thy triumph. But being pure cast aside all fear; for the hour is often terrible, a fire and a whirlwind and a tempest, a treading of the winepress of the wrath of God; but he who can stand up in it on the truth of his purpose is he who shall stand; even though he fall, he shall rise again, even though he seem to pass on the wings of the wind, he shall return. Nor let worldly prudence whisper too closely in thy ear; for it is the hour of the unexpected.[68]

SRI AUROBINDO

9. THE GOSPEL OF FAITH

The Fundamental Faith

Faith does not depend upon experience; it is something that is there before experience. When one starts the yoga, it is not usually on the strength of experience, but on the strength of faith. It is so not only in yoga and the spiritual life, but in ordinary life also. All men of action, discoverers, inventors, creators of knowledge proceed by faith and, until the proof is made or the thing done, they go on in spite of disappointment, failure, disproof, denial because of something in them that tells them that this is the truth, the thing that must be followed and done. Ramakrishna even went so far as to say, when asked whether blind faith was not wrong, that blind faith was the only kind to have, for faith is either blind or it is not faith but something else — reasoned inference, proved conviction or ascertained knowledge.

Faith is the soul's witness to something not yet manifested, achieved or realised, but which yet the Knower within us, even in the absence of all indications, feels to be true or supremely worth following or achieving. This thing within us can last even when there is no fixed belief in the mind, even when the vital struggles and revolts and refuses. Who is there that practises the yoga and has not his periods, long periods of disappointment and failure and disbelief and darkness? But there is something that sustains him and even goes on in spite of himself, because it feels that what it followed after was yet true and it more than feels, it knows. The fundamental faith in yoga is this, inherent in the soul, that the Divine exists and the Divine is the one thing to be followed after — nothing else in life is worth having in comparison with that. So long as a man has that faith, he is marked for the spiritual life and I will say that, even if his nature is full of obstacles and crammed with denials and difficulties, and even if he has many years of struggle, he is marked out for success in the spiritual life.

It is this faith that you need to develop — a faith which is in accordance with reason and common sense — that if the Divine exists and has called you to the Path, (as is evident), then there must be a Divine Guidance behind and through and in spite of all difficulties you will arrive. Not to listen to the hostile voices that suggest failure or to the voices of impatient, vital haste that echo them, not to believe that because great difficulties are there, there can be no success or that because the Divine has not yet shown himself he will never show himself, but to take the position that everyone takes when he fixes his mind on a great and difficult goal, "I will go on till I succeed — all difficulties notwithstanding." To which the believer in the Divine adds, "The Divine exists, my following after the Divine cannot fail. I will go on through everything till I find him." [69]

SRI AUROBINDO

The Central Faith

Even a faltering faith and a slow and partial surrender have their force and their result, otherwise only the rare few could do sadhana at all. What I mean by the central faith is a faith in the soul or the central being behind, a faith which is there even when the mind doubts and the vital despairs and the physical wants to collapse, and after the attack is over reappears and pushes on the path again. It may be strong and bright, it may be pale and in appearance weak, but if it persists each time in going on, it is the real thing. Fits of depression and darkness and despair are a tradition in the path of sadhana — in all yogas oriental or occidental they seem to have been the rule. I know all about them myself — but my experience has led me to the perception that they are an unnecessary tradition and could be dispensed with if one chose. That is why whenever they come in you or others I try to lift up before them the gospel of faith. If still they come, one has to get through them as soon as possible and get back into the sun.[70]

SRI AUROBINDO

Faith and Trust Both Needed

There is a second [thing], which is obviously, as indispensable if you want to go forward; it is to have faith. Or another word, which seems more limited but is for me more important, because (it is a question of experience) if your faith is not made of a complete trust in the Divine, well, you may very easily remain under the impression that you have faith and yet be losing all trust in the divine Power or divine Goodness, or the Trust the Divine has in you. These are the three stumbling-blocks:

Those who have what they call an unshakable faith in the Divine, and say, "It is the Divine who is doing everything, who can do everything; all that happens in me, in others, everywhere, is the work of the Divine and the Divine alone", if they follow this with some kind of logic, after some time they will blame the Divine for all the most terrible wrongs which take place in the world and make of Him a real demon, cruel and frightful — if they have no trust.

Or again, they do have faith, but tell themselves, "Well, I have faith in the Divine, but this world, I see quite well what it's like! First of all, I suffer so much, don't I? I am very unhappy, far more unhappy than all my neighbours" — for one is always far more unhappy than all one's neighbours — "I am very unhappy and, truly, life is cruel to me. But then the Divine is divine, He is All-Goodness, All-Generosity, All-Harmony, so how is it that I am so unhappy? He must be powerless; otherwise being so good how could He let me suffer so much?"

That is the second stumbling-block.

And the third: there are people who have what may be called a warped and excessive modesty or humility and who tell themselves, "Surely the Divine has thrown me out, I am good for nothing, He can do nothing with me, the only thing for me is to give up the game, for He finds me unworthy of Him!"

So, unless one adds to faith a total and complete trust in the Divine Grace, there will be difficulties. So both are necessary.[71]

THE MOTHER

What are the conditions in which there is a descent of faith?

The most important condition is an almost childlike trust, the candid trust of a child who is sure that it will come, who doesn't even ask himself about it; when he needs something he is sure that it is going to come. Well, it is this, this kind of trust — this indeed is the most important condition.

To aspire is indispensable. But some people aspire with such a conflict inside them between faith and absence of faith, trust and distrust, between the optimism which is sure of victory and a pessimism which asks itself when the catastrophe will come. Now if this is in the being, you may aspire but you don't get anything. And you say, "I aspired but didn't get anything." It is because you demolish your aspiration all the time by your lack of confidence. But if you truly have trust... Children when left to themselves and not deformed by older people have such a great trust that all will be well! For example, when they have a small accident, they never think that this is going to be something serious: they are spontaneously convinced that it will soon be over, and this helps so powerfully in putting an end to it.

Well, when one aspires for the Force, when one asks the Divine for help, if one asks with the unshakable certitude that it will come, that it is impossible that it won't, then it is sure to come. It is this kind... yes, this is truly an inner opening, this trustfulness. And some people are constantly in this state. When there is something to be received, they are always there to receive it. There are others, when there is something to have, a force descends, they are always absent, they are always closed at that moment; while those who have this childlike trust are always there at the right time.

And it is strange, isn't it, outwardly there is no difference. They may have exactly the same goodwill, the same aspiration, the same wish to do good, but those who have this smiling confidence within them, do not question, do not ask themselves whether they will have it or not have it, whether the Divine will answer or not — the question does not arise, it is something understood... "What I need will be given to me; if I pray I shall have an answer; if I am in a difficulty and ask for help, the help will come — and not only will it come but it will manage everything." If the trust is there, spontaneous, candid, unquestioning, it works better than anything else, and the results are marvellous. It is with the contradictions and doubts of the mind that one spoils everything, with this kind of notion which comes when one is in difficulties: "Oh, it is impossible! I shall never manage it. And if it is going to be aggravated, if this condition I am in, which I don't want, is going to grow still worse, if I continue to slide down farther and farther, if, if, if, if..." like that, and one builds a wall between oneself and the force one wants to receive. The psychic being has this trust, has it wonderfully, without a shadow, without an argument, without a contradiction. And when it is like that, there is not a prayer which does not get an answer, no aspiration which is not realised.[72]

THE MOTHER

Preserving Faith

Sweet Mother, can faith be increased by personal effort?

Faith is certainly a gift given to us by the Divine Grace. It is like a door suddenly opening upon an eternal truth, through which we can see it, almost touch it.

As in everything else in the ascent of humanity, there is the necessity — especially at the beginning — of personal effort. It is possible that in some exceptional circumstances, for reasons which completely elude our intelligence, faith may come almost accidentally, quite unexpectedly, almost without ever having been solicited, but most frequently it is an answer to a yearning, a need, an aspiration, something in the being that is seeking and longing, even though not in a very conscious and systematic way. But in any case, when faith has been granted, when one has had this sudden inner illumination, in order to preserve it constantly in the active consciousness individual effort is altogether indispensable. One must *hold on* to one's faith, *will* one's faith; one must seek it, cultivate it, protect it.

In the human mind there is a morbid and deplorable habit of doubt, argument, scepticism. *This* is where human effort must be put in: the refusal to admit them, the refusal to listen to them and still more the refusal to follow them. No game is more dangerous than playing mentally with doubt and scepticism. They are not only enemies, they are terrible pitfalls, and once one falls into them, it becomes tremendously difficult to pull oneself out.

Some people think it is a very great mental elegance

to play with ideas, to discuss them, to contradict their faith; they think that this gives them a very superior attitude, that in this way they are above "superstitions" and "ignorance"; but if you listen to suggestions of doubt and scepticism, *then* you fall into the grossest ignorance and stray away from the right path. You enter into confusion, error, a maze of contradictions.... You are not always sure you will be able to get out of it. You go so far away from the inner truth that you lose sight of it and sometimes lose too all possible contact with your soul.

Certainly a personal effort is needed to preserve one's faith, to let it grow within. Later — much later — one day, looking back, we may see that everything that happened, even what seemed to us the worst, was a Divine Grace to make us advance on the way; and then we become aware that the personal effort too was a grace. But before reaching that point, one has to advance much, to struggle much, sometimes even to suffer a great deal.

To sit down in inert passivity and say, "If I am to have faith I shall have it, the Divine will give it to me", is an attitude of laziness, of unconsciousness and almost of bad-will.

For the inner flame to burn, one must feed it; one must watch over the fire, throw into it the fuel of all the errors one wants to get rid of, all that delays the progress, all that darkens the path. If one doesn't feed the fire, it smoulders under the ashes of one's unconsciousness and inertia, and then, not years but lives, centuries will pass before one reaches the goal.

One must watch over one's faith as one watches over the birth of something *infinitely* precious, and protect it very carefully from everything that can impair it.

In the ignorance and darkness of the beginning, faith is the most direct expression of the Divine Power which comes to fight and conquer.[73]

THE MOTHER

He Who Chooses the Infinite

The lotus of the eternal knowledge and the eternal perfection is a bud closed and folded up within us. It opens swiftly or gradually, petal by petal, through successive realisations, once the mind of man begins to turn towards the Eternal, once his heart, no longer compressed and confined by attachment to finite appearances, becomes enamoured, in whatever degree, of the Infinite. All life, all thought, all energising of the faculties, all experiences passive or active, become thenceforward so many shocks which disintegrate the teguments of the soul and remove the obstacles to the inevitable efflorescence. He who chooses the Infinite has been chosen by the Infinite. He has received the divine touch without which there is no awakening, no opening of the spirit; but once it is received, attainment is sure, whether conquered swiftly in the course of one human life or pursued patiently through many stadia of the cycle of existence in the manifested universe.[74]

SRI AUROBINDO

> He who chooses the Infinite has been chosen by the infinite.
> — *Sri Aurobindo*

It is a magnificent sentence!

And it is absolutely true. There is in *Thoughts and Glimpses* also a sentence like this where I think he uses the word "God" instead of the Infinite. But the idea is the same — that it is God who has chosen you, the Divine who has chosen you. And that is why you run after Him!

And this is what gives — that's what he says, doesn't he? — this is what gives that kind of confidence, of certitude, precisely, that one is predestined; and if one is predestined, even if there are mountains of difficulties, what can that matter since one is sure to succeed! This gives you an indomitable courage to face all difficulties and a patience that stands all trials: you are sure to succeed.

And it's a fact — in fact, it is like that: the moment you thought about it, well, you thought about it because someone thought about you; you chose because you were chosen. And once you have been chosen, you are sure of the thing. Therefore, doubts, hesitations, depressions, uncertainties, all this is quite simply a waste of time and energy; it is of no use at all.

From the moment one has felt just once within himself: "Ah! *This* is the truth for me", it is finished; it is finished, it is settled. Even if you spend years cutting your way through the virgin forest, it's of no importance — it is finished, it is settled.

That is why I told you one day, "After all, you all are here because you have wanted it somewhere; and if you wanted it somewhere, it means that the Divine wanted it thus in you."

So there are some who follow a very straight path and arrive very quickly; there are others who love labyrinths, it takes longer. But the end is there, the goal is there. I know by experience that there isn't one being who, were it only once in his life, has had a great urge towards... it doesn't matter what he calls it — let us say the Divine for facility of speech, who is not sure to arrive; even if he turns his back on Him at a certain time, it's of no importance — he is sure to arrive. He will have to struggle more or less, will have more or less difficulty, but he is sure to succeed one day. It's a soul that has been chosen, it has become conscious because its hour has come — once the hour has come, well, the result will follow more or less quickly. You can do this in a few months; you can do it in some years; you can do it in some lives — but you will do it.

And what is remarkable is that this freedom of choice is left to you and that, if you decide within yourself that you will do it in this lifetime, you will do it. And I am not speaking here of a permanent and continuous decision because then you can arrive in twelve months. No, I mean: if you have suddenly been seized by this, "I want this", even once, in a flash, the seal is put, there, like that.

There we are.

That's not a reason for wasting time on the way; that's not a reason for just following all the meanderings of the labyrinth and arriving with... with considerable rubbish when you are at the end. No. But, in any case it is a reason for never despairing, whatever the difficulties may be.

I am of the opinion that when there is something to

do, it is better to do it as quickly as possible. But still, there are people who like to waste their time. Perhaps they need to turn and turn and turn and return and make lots of windings before reaching the place they have to. But that's a question of choice. Unfortunately, those who are in this habit of turning and returning and turning aside and making all kinds of useless meanderings, are the ones who complain most; they moan, and they are the workers of their own misery!

If one decided to go quite straight upon his path, whatever the cost — knowing how to bear a few difficulties, facing discomforts, without weakness, you see — well, one would avoid much trouble. But some people go only if they are taken by the scruff of the neck and dragged with a terrible force. Then they shout that they are violently forced.[75]

THE MOTHER

Does the Supreme choose the being who will be his instrument, or does the being choose to become his instrument?

You can take it as you like.

One can't tell who began! But the two usually take place at the same time.

If you want an order of priority, it is evident that the Divine exists before the individual, so it must be the Divine who has chosen first! But that is a choice prior to terrestrial life. In the order of the ordinary human consciousness it may be one or the other or both at the same time. In fact, it is likely that the Divine is the first to notice that this or that being is ready! But he who is ready generally does not know it to begin with, so he has the impression that it is he who has decided and is choosing. But this is more of an impression than a reality.

And once you are chosen, it is ineluctable, you can't escape even if you try.[76]

THE MOTHER

The Constant Mantra

If you desire only the Divine, there is an absolute certitude that you will reach the Divine, but all these questionings and repinings at each movement only delay and keep an impending curtain before the heart and the eyes. For at every step, when one makes an advance, the opposite forces will throw these doubts like a rope between the legs and stop one short with a stumble — it is their *métier* to do that.... One must say, "Since I want only the Divine, my success is sure, I have only to walk forward in all confidence and His own Hand will be there secretly leading me to Him by His own way and at His own time." That is what you must keep as your constant mantra. Anything else one may doubt but that he who desires only the Divine shall reach the Divine is a certitude and more certain than two and two make four. That is the faith every sadhak must have at the bottom of his heart, supporting him through every stumble and blow and ordeal.[77]

SRI AUROBINDO

The Goal is Sure

If you are in a state of conscious aspiration and very sincere, well, everything around you will be arranged in order to help in your aspiration, whether directly or indirectly, that is, either to make you progress, put you in touch with something new or to eliminate from your nature something that has to disappear. This is something quite remarkable. If you are truly in a state of intensity of aspiration, there is not a circumstance which does not come to help you to realise this aspiration. Everything comes, everything, as though there were a perfect and absolute consciousness organising around you all things, and you yourself in your outer ignorance may not recognise it and may protest at first against the circumstances as they show themselves, may complain, may try to change them; but after a while, when you have become wiser, and there is a certain distance between you and the event, well, you will realise that it was just what you needed to do to make the necessary progress. And, you know, it is a will, a supreme goodwill which arranges all things around you, and even when you complain and protest instead of accepting, it is exactly at such moments that it acts most effectively.

I have written a short sentence* which will appear in the *Bulletin*, the next *Bulletin*. It goes something like this (I don't remember the words exactly now): If you say to the Divine with conviction, "I want only You", the Divine will arrange all the circumstances in such a way as to compel

* "If earnestly you say to the Divine, 'I want only Thee', the Divine will arrange the circumstances in such a way that you are compelled to be sincere."

you to be sincere. Something in the being... "I want only You."... the aspiration... and then one wants a hundred odd things all the time, isn't that so? At times something comes, just... usually to disturb everything — it stands in the way and prevents you from realising your aspiration. Well, the Divine will come without showing Himself, without your seeing Him, without your having any inkling of it, and He will arrange all the circumstances in such a way that everything that prevents you from belonging solely to the Divine will be removed from your path, inevitably. Then when all is removed, you begin to howl and complain; but later, if you are sincere and look at yourself straight in the eye... you have said to the Lord, you have said, "I want only You." He will remain close to you, all the rest will go away. This is indeed a higher Grace. Only, you must say this with conviction. I don't even mean that you must say it integrally, because if one says it integrally, the work is done. What is necessary is that one part of the being, indeed the central will, says it with conviction: "I want only You." Even once, and it suffices: all that takes more or less long, sometimes it stretches over years, but one reaches the goal.

But one has all kinds of imperfections!

Eh? The more the imperfections, the longer it takes; the more the attachments one has, the longer it takes.

BUT THE GOAL IS SURE![78]

THE MOTHER

10. A NEW WORLD IS BORN, BORN, BORN

It is quite difficult to free oneself from old habits of being and to be able to freely conceive of a new life, a new world. And naturally, the liberation begins on the highest planes of consciousness: it is easier for the mind or the higher intelligence to conceive of new things than for the vital being, for instance, to feel things in a new way. And it is still more difficult for the body to have a purely material perception of what a new world will be. Yet this perception must *precede* the material transformation; first one must *feel* very concretely the strangeness of the old things, their lack of relevance, if I may say so. One must have the feeling, even a material impression, that they are outdated, that they belong to a past which no longer has any purpose. For the old impressions one had of past things which have become historic — which have their interest from that point of view and support the advance of the present and the future — this is still a movement that belongs to the old world: it is the old world that is unfolding with a past, a present, a future. But for the creation of a new world, there is, so to speak, only a continuity of transition which gives an appearance — an impression rather — the impression of two things still intermingled but almost disconnected, and that the things of the past no longer have the power or the strength to endure, with whatever modifications, in the new things. That other world is necessarily an *absolutely* new experience. One would have to go back to the time when there was a transition from the animal to the human creation to find a similar period, and at that time the consciousness was not sufficiently mentalised to be able to observe, understand, feel intelligently — the passage must have been made in a completely obscure way. So, what I am speaking about is absolutely new, *unique* in the terrestrial creation, it is something unprecedented, truly a perception or a sensation or an impression... that is quite strange and new. (*After a silence*) A disconnection: something which has overstayed its time and has only quite a subordinate force of existence, from something totally new, but still so young, so imperceptible, almost weak, so to say; it hasn't yet the power to impose and assert itself and to predominate, to take the place of the other. So there is a concomitance but, as I said, with a disconnection, that is, the connection between the two is missing.

It is difficult to describe, but I am speaking to you about it because this is what I felt yesterday evening. I felt it so acutely... that it made me look at certain things, and once I had seen them I felt it would be interesting to tell you about them.

(*Silence*)

It seems strange that something so new, so special and I might say so unexpected should happen during a film-show.* For people who believe that some things are important and other things are not, that there are activities which are helpful to yoga and others which are not, well, this is

* A Bengali film, *Rani Rasmani*, which describes the lives of Sri Ramakrishna and Rani Rasmani, a rich, very intelligent and religious Bengali widow, who in 1847 built the temple of Kali at Dakshineshwar (Bengal) where Sri Ramakrishna lived and worshipped Kali.

one more opportunity to show that they are wrong. I have always noticed that it is unexpected things which give you the most interesting experiences.

Yesterdayevening,suddenly something happened which I have just described to you as best I could — I don't know if I have succeeded in making myself understood — but it was truly quite new and altogether unexpected. We were shown, comparatively clumsily, a picture of the temple on the banks of the Ganges, and the statue of Kali — for I suppose it was a photograph of that statue, I could not manage to get any precise information about it — and while I was seeing that, which was a completely superficial appearance and, as I said, rather clumsy, I saw the reality it was trying to represent, what was behind, and this put me in touch with all that world of religion and worship, of aspiration, man's whole relationship with the gods, which was — I am already speaking in the past tense — which was the flower of the human spiritual effort towards something more divine than man, something which was the highest and almost the purest expression of his effort towards what is higher than he. And suddenly I had *concretely, materially*, the impression that it was another world, a world that had ceased to be real, living, an outdated world which had lost its reality, its truth, which had been transcended, surpassed by something which had taken birth and was only beginning to express itself, but whose *life* was *so intense*, so true, so sublime, that all this became false, unreal, worthless.

Then I truly understood — for I understood not with the head, the intelligence but with the body, you understand what I mean — I understood in the cells of the body — that a new world *is born* and is beginning to grow....

Well, I announced* to you all that this new world was born. But it has been so engulfed, as it were, in the old world that so far the difference has not been very perceptible to many people. Still, the action of the new forces has continued very regularly, very persistently, very steadily, and to a certain extent, very effectively. And one of the manifestations of this action was my experience — truly so very new — of yesterday evening. And the result of all this I have noted step by step in almost daily experiences. It could be expressed succinctly, in a rather linear way:

First, it is not only a "new conception" of spiritual life and the divine Reality. This conception was expressed by Sri Aurobindo, I have expressed it myself many a time, and it could be formulated somewhat like this: the old spirituality was an escape from life into the divine Reality, leaving the world just where it was, as it was; whereas our new vision, on the contrary, is a divinisation of life, a transformation of the material world into a divine world. This has been said, repeated, more or less understood, indeed it is the basic idea of what we want to do. But this could be a continuation with an improvement, a widening of the old world as it was — and so long as this is a conception up there in the field of thought, in fact it is hardly more than that — but what has happened, the really new thing, is that a new world is *born, born, born.* It is not the old one transforming itself, it is a *new* world which is *born.* And we are right in the midst of this period of transition where the two are entangled —

* The Mother had announced that on 29 February, 1956 there took place what she called "the first Manifestation of the Supramental Light-Force in the earth atmosphere". — Ed.

where the other still persists all-powerful and entirely dominating the ordinary consciousness, but where the new one is quietly slipping in, still very modest, unnoticed — unnoticed to the extent that outwardly it doesn't disturb anything very much, for the time being, and that in the consciousness of most people it is even altogether imperceptible. And yet it is working, growing — until it is strong enough to assert itself visibly.

In any case, to simplify things, it could be said that characteristically the old world, the creation of what Sri Aurobindo calls the Overmind, was an age of the gods, and consequently the age of religions. As I said, the flower of human effort towards what is above it gave rise to innumerable religious forms, to a religious relationship between the best souls and the invisible world. And at the very summit of all that, as an effort towards a higher realisation there has arisen the idea of the unity of religions, of this "one single thing" which is behind all these manifestations; and this idea has truly been, so to speak, the extreme limit of human aspiration. Well, that is at the frontier, it is something that still belongs *completely* to the Overmind world, the Overmind creation and which from there seems to be looking towards this "other thing" which is a new creation it cannot grasp — which it tries to reach, feels coming, but cannot grasp. To grasp it, a reversal is needed. It is necessary to leave the Overmind creation. It was necessary that the new creation, the supramental creation should take place.

And now, all these old things seem so old, so out-of-date, so arbitrary — such a travesty of the real truth.

In the supramental creation there will *no longer be any religions.* The whole life will be the expression, the flowering into forms of the divine Unity manifesting in the world. And there will no longer be what men now call gods.

These great divine beings themselves will be able to participate in the new creation; but to do so, they will have to put on what we could call the "supramental substance" on earth. And if some of them choose to remain in their world as they are, if they decide not to manifest physically, their relation with the beings of a supramental earth will be a relation of friends, collaborators, equals, for the highest divine essence will be manifested in the beings of the new supramental world on earth.

When the physical substance is supramentalised, to incarnate on earth will no longer be a cause of inferiority, quite the contrary. It will give a plenitude which cannot be obtained otherwise.

But all this is in the future; it is a future... which has *begun*, but which will take some time to be realised integrally. Meanwhile we are in a very special situation, extremely special, without precedent. We are now witnessing the birth of a new world; it is very young, very weak — not in its essence but in its outer manifestation — not yet recognised, not even felt, denied by the majority. But it is here. It is here, making an effort to grow, absolutely *sure* of the result. But the road to it is a completely new road which has never before been traced out — nobody has gone there, nobody has done that! It is a beginning, a *universal beginning*. So, it is an absolutely unexpected and unpredictable adventure.[79]

THE MOTHER

Manifestation of the Supermind

In fact, a supermind is already here but it is involved, concealed behind this manifest mind, life and Matter and not yet acting overtly or in its own power: if it acts, it is through these inferior powers and modified by their characters and so not yet recognisable. It is only by the approach and arrival of the descending Supermind that it can be liberated upon earth and reveal itself in the action of our material, vital and mental parts so that these lower powers can become portions of a total divinised activity of our whole being: it is that that will bring to us a completely realised divinity or the divine life. It is indeed so that life and mind involved in Matter have realised themselves here; for only what is involved can evolve, otherwise there could be no emergence.

— *Sri Aurobindo*

Sweet Mother, what is the involved supermind?

It is the same as the uninvolved one! It is the same thing when Sri Aurobindo says that if the Divine were not at the centre of everything, He could never manifest in the world; it is the same thing when he says that essentially, in its origin and deepest structure, the creation is divine, the world is divine; and that is why this divinity will be able to manifest one day, become tangible, express itself fully in place of all that veils and deforms it at present. Up to now, all that has manifested of this divinity is the world as we know it; but the manifestation is boundless, and after this mental world as we know it, of which the apex and prototype is man, another reality will manifest, which Sri Aurobindo calls the Supermind, for it is in fact the next step after the mind; so, seen from the world as it is, it will naturally be "supramental", that is, something above the mind. And he also says that it will truly be the changing of one world into another, for so far the whole creation belonged to what he calls "the lower hemisphere" as we know it, which is governed by Ignorance and based upon the Inconscient, whereas the other one will be a complete reversal, the sudden appearance of something which will belong to quite a different world, and which instead of being based on Ignorance will be based upon Truth. That is why it will truly be a new world. But if the *essence*, the principle of this world were not included in the world as we knew it, there would be no hope of the one being transformed into the other; they would be two worlds so totally different and opposed that there would be no contact between them and that necessarily, as soon as one came out of this world and emerged into the world of Truth, Light and Knowledge, one would become, so to speak, imperceptible, non-existent for a world belonging exclusively to the Ignorance and the Inconscience.

How is it that even when this change has taken place, there will be a connection and this new world will be able to act upon the old one? It is that in its essence and principle the new is already enclosed, involved in the old world. So, in fact, it is there, inside, in its very depths, hidden, invisible, imperceptible, unexpressed, but it is there, in its essence. Still, unless from the supreme heights the supramental consciousness and force and light manifest directly in the world, as it happened a year and a half ago, this Supermind which in *principle* is at the very bedrock of the material world as it is, would never have any possibility of manifesting itself. Its awakening and appearance below will be the response to a touch from above which will bring out the corresponding element hidden in the depths of matter as it is now.... And this is precisely what is happening at present. But as I told you two weeks ago, this material world as it actually, visibly is, is so powerful, so absolutely real for the ordinary consciousness, that it has engulfed, as it were, this supramental force and consciousness when it manifested, and a long preparation is necessary before its presence can be even glimpsed, felt, perceived in some way or other. And this is the work it is doing now.

How long it will take is difficult to foresee. It will depend a great deal on the goodwill and the receptivity of a certain number of people, for the individual always advances faster than the collectivity, and by its very nature, humanity is destined to manifest the Supermind before the rest of creation.

At the basis of this collaboration there is necessarily the will to change, no longer to be what one is, for things to be no longer what they are. There are several ways of reaching it, and all the methods are good when they succeed! One may be deeply disgusted with what exists and wish ardently to come out of all this and attain something else; one may — and this is a more positive way — one may feel within oneself the touch, the approach of something positively beautiful and true, and willingly drop all the rest so that nothing may burden the journey to this new beauty and truth.

What is indispensable in every case is the *ardent* will for progress, the willing and joyful renunciation of all that hampers the advance: to throw far away from oneself all that prevents one from going forward, and to set out into the unknown with the ardent faith that this is the truth of tomorrow, *inevitable,* which must necessarily come, which nothing, nobody, no bad will, even that of Nature, can prevent from becoming a reality — perhaps of a not too distant future — a reality which is being worked out now and which those who know how to change, how not to be weighed down by old habits, will *surely* have the good fortune not only to see but to realise.[80]

THE MOTHER

Passing into the Supramental Consciousness

As the beginnings of the supramental life, which must be the next realisation in the unfolding of the universe, develop, perhaps not in a very obvious way but very surely, it becomes more and more obvious that the most difficult way to approach this supramental life is intellectual activity.

It could be said that it is much more difficult to pass from the mental to the supramental life than to pass from a certain psychic emotion in life — something that is like a reflection, a luminous emanation of the divine Presence in matter — to the supramental consciousness; it is much easier to pass from that into the supramental consciousness than to pass from the highest intellectual speculation to any supramental vibration. Perhaps it is the word that misleads us! Perhaps it is because we call it "supramental" that we expect to reach it through a higher intellectual mental activity? But the fact is very different. With this very high, very pure, very noble intellectual activity, one seems to move towards a kind of cold, powerless abstraction, a frozen, an icy light which is surely very remote from life and still further away from the experience of the supramental reality.

In this new substance which is spreading and acting in the world, there is a warmth, a power, a joy so intense that all intellectual activity seems cold and dry beside it. And that is why the less one talks about these things the better it is. A single moment, a single impulse of deep and true love, an instant of the understanding which lies in the divine Grace brings you much closer to the goal than all possible explanations.

Even a kind of refined sensation, subtle, clear, luminous, acute, which penetrates deep, opens the door for you more than the subtlest explanations.

And if we carry the experience still further, it seems that when one comes to the work of transformation of the body, when some cells of the body, more ready than others, more refined, more subtle, more plastic, are able to feel concretely the presence of the divine Grace, the divine Will, the divine Power, this Knowledge that is not intellectual but a knowledge by identity, when one feels this in the cells of the body, then the experience is so total, so imperative, so living, concrete, tangible, real that everything else seems a vain dream.

And so we may say that it is truly when the circle is complete and the two extremities touch, when the highest manifests in the most material, that the experience will be truly conclusive.

It seems that one can never truly understand until one understands with one's body.[81]

THE MOTHER

Action of the Supramental Force and Individual Effort

Mother, this new force which is going to act, will it act through individual effort or independently of it?

Why this opposition? It acts independently of all individual effort, as if automatically in the world, but it *creates* individual effort and *makes use* of it. Individual effort is one of its means of action, and perhaps the most powerful. If one thinks that individual effort is due to the individual, it is an illusion, but if the individual under the pretext that there is a universal action independent of himself refuses to make an individual effort, he refuses to give his collaboration. The Force wants to use, and does in fact use individual effort as one of the most powerful means at its disposal. It is the Force itself, it is this Power which *is* your individual effort.

And so, you see, the first movement of vital self-conceit when it is told, "You don't exist in yourself", naturally it says, "All right, I won't do anything any more! I am not the one who works, so I won't work any longer" and "Very good, the Divine can do everything, it is his business, I won't stir any more. If the credit does not go to me"—it comes to that—"I won't do anything any more." Well! But indeed there's no word for such things. This is something I constantly hear, it is simply a way of venting one's offended self-conceit, that's all. But the true reaction, the pure reaction is an enthusiastic impulse of collaboration, to play the game with all the energy, the will-power at the disposal of one's consciousness, in the state one is in, with the feeling of being supported, carried by something infinitely greater than oneself, which makes no mistakes, something which protects you and at the same time gives you all the necessary strength and uses you as the best instrument. And one feels that, and one feels one is working in security, that one can no longer make any mistakes, that what one does is done with the utmost result and — in delight. That is the true movement; to feel that one's will is intensified to the utmost because it is no longer a tiny little microscopic person in infinity but an infinite universal Power which makes you act: the Force of Truth. This is the only true reaction.[82]

THE MOTHER

The New Birth — The Decisive Step

... when people tell me, "I would like to know whether I am in contact with my soul or not", I say, "If you ask the question, that is enough to prove that you are not. You don't need an answer, you are giving it to yourself." When it is *that*, it is that, and then it is finished, it is no longer anything else.

And since we are speaking of that, I shall remind you of what Sri Aurobindo has said, repeated, written, affirmed and said over and over again, that his yoga, the integral yoga, can begin *only after* that experience, not before.

So, one must not cherish any illusions and fancy that one can begin to know what the supermind is and form any idea of it or assess it in any way, however minimal, before having had *that* experience.

Therefore, if you want to advance on the path, you must very modestly start on your way towards the new birth, first, and realise it before cherishing the illusion that you can have supramental experiences.

To console you I may tell you that by the very fact that you live on earth at this time — whether you are conscious of it or not, even whether you want it or not — you are absorbing with the air you breathe this new supramental substance which is now spreading in the earth atmosphere. And it is preparing things in you which will manifest *very suddenly*, as soon as you have taken the decisive step.

(*Silence*)

Whether this will help you to take the decisive step or not is another question which remains to be studied, for the experiences which are occurring and will occur more and more frequently now, being of a radically new kind, we can't know beforehand what is going to happen; we must study, and after a thorough study we shall be able to say with certainty whether this supramental substance makes the work of new birth easier or not.... I shall tell you this a little later. For the moment it is better not to rely on these things and, very simply, to start on your way to be born into the spiritual life.

When this happens to you, almost all the questions you ask yourself or ask me will be solved.

And anyway, your attitude to life will be *so* different that you will understand what is meant when one speaks of living spiritually. And at that moment you will also understand a *great* thing, a very great thing: how to live without ego.

Until then, you cannot understand it. The whole of

life is so dependent on the ego that it seems absolutely impossible to live and act except with or by the ego, but after this new birth you can look at the ego with a smile and say to it, "My friend, I don't need you any more."

This is also one of the results which brings you a very decisive sense of liberation.[83]

THE MOTHER

Living a Miracle

I don't know if you have had this experience, when reading one of the wonderful stories of mankind, and of those who came to help humanity — you have perhaps heard this more here in India than people in other countries — those stories in which there was an intervention from above, there was one of those chances, one of those miraculous Graces.

And so, if one reads that when one is small, one says, "Oh, how I should like to have lived at that time!" — I don't know if you have had this experience...

I knew people who had it. And then one tells them, "Well, try to imagine that you have it, this chance, what would be your reaction?" And sometimes suddenly one perceives it; suddenly it seems as if the heavens were opened, and that something has come which was not there before. For how long, one can't say, but in any case, it is one of those extraordinary moments of earth-life and human life when things are not as they ordinarily are, dull and lifeless. So one has the feeling of living a miracle.

If one can keep this, all goes well. Unfortunately one forgets it very quickly.

If one has had it once, it is already something; the door has been opened. Suddenly one has felt... yes, felt, it is something, it is an infinite Grace, it is something marvellous. All those who lived a century ago, two centuries ago, three centuries ago, hoped for it, awaited it. They had only one chance, that was to live again in a new life and in better conditions.

But now, we have these conditions, they are here: the Grace is here.

If one can manage to have the experience — not only a thought — the experience of the thing, and then keep it afterwards, then all becomes easy. Unfortunately, one forgets very soon.[84]

THE MOTHER

The Most Important Thing

People sleep, they forget, they take life easy — they forget, forget all the time.... But if we could remember... that we are at an exceptional hour, a *unique* time, that we have this immense good fortune, this invaluable privilege of being present at the birth of a new world, we could easily get rid of everything that impedes and hinders our progress.

So, the most important thing, it seems, is to remember this fact; even when one doesn't have the tangible experience, to have the certainty of it and faith in it; to remember always, to recall it constantly, to go to sleep with this idea, to wake up with this perception; to do all that one does with this great truth as the background, as a constant support, this great truth that we are witnessing the birth of a new world.

We can participate in it, we can become this new world. And truly, when one has such a marvellous opportunity, one should be ready to give up everything for its sake."[85]

THE MOTHER

The Most Essential Condition

It is then by a transformation of life in its very principle, not by an external manipulation of its phenomena, that the integral Yoga proposes to change it from a troubled and ignorant into a luminous and harmonious movement of Nature. There are three conditions which are indispensable for the achievement of this central inner revolution and a new formation; none of them is altogether sufficient in itself, but by their united threefold power the uplifting can be done, the conversion made and completely made. For, first, life as it is is a movement of desire and it has built in us as its centre a desire-soul which refers to itself all the motions of life and puts in them its own troubled hue and pain of an ignorant, half-lit, baffled endeavour: for a divine living, desire must be abolished and replaced by a purer and firmer motive-power, the tormented soul of desire dissolved and in its stead there must emerge the calm, strength, happiness of a true vital being now concealed within us. Next, life as it is is driven or led partly by the impulse of the life-force, partly by a mind which is mostly a servant and abettor of the ignorant life-impulse, but in part also its uneasy and not too luminous or competent guide and mentor; for a divine life the mind and the life-impulse

> must cease to be anything but instruments and the inmost psychic being must take their place as the leader on the path and the indicator of a divine guidance. Last, life as it is is turned towards the satisfaction of the separative ego; ego must disappear and be replaced by the true spiritual person, the central being, and life itself must be turned towards the fulfilment of the Divine in terrestrial existence; it must feel a Divine Force awaking within it and become an obedient instrumentation of its purpose.
>
> Sri Aurobindo, *The Synthesis of Yoga*, p. 166

What I read today seems to be the most essential condition for starting, because it is the most universal.

(*After a silence*) Everyone must follow his path in accordance with his own nature, and there is always a preference for one way rather than another. As we read in one of our recent classes, for one who follows the path of action, it is much more difficult to feel that the human personality does not exist and that only the divine Force works. For one who follows the path of knowledge it is relatively very easy, it is something one discovers almost immediately. For one who follows the path of love it is elementary, since it is by giving himself that he progresses. But for one who follows the path of action it is much more difficult, and consequently for him the first step is to do what is said here in the passage of *The Synthesis of Yoga* which we have just read: to create in himself this complete detachment from the fruit of action, to act because this is what must be done, to do it in the best possible way, and not to be anxious about the consequences, to leave the consequences to a Will higher than his own.

One can't make a general rule for the order of importance of the paths, it is an exclusively personal affair. And there is a time when one understands very well, it is apparent, that no two paths are alike, no two paths can be alike, and that every man follows his own path and that this is the truth of his being. One can, if one looks from a sufficient height, see a difference in the speed of advance, but it does not always conform to the external signs; and one could say a little humorously, that it is not always the wisest who goes fastest!

(*Silence*)

It seems to me no longer possible to make general rules. Indeed, the Grace is upon all. And what is necessary to let it act? It is very difficult to say.

If one can see it, feel it, experience its action, so to say, be conscious of its presence and movement, then one has the joy of the movement, the progress, the realisation; but this does not mean that if one doesn't feel this joy, the action of the Grace is not there, the realisation not there.

And after all, all the ways of being of the Divine, all the forms of being in the manifestation are necessary to express the Divine. It is this manifestation as a whole, in its totality, which progresses towards a growing, infinite, eternal perfection. It is not each separate element, individually, it is all together, as a collective and total expression of the divine Truth. All this is moving forward constantly, eternally, towards a greater perfection. The universe of tomorrow will necessarily be more divine, if one may say so, than the universe of yesterday; and that of yesterday was more divine than the one preceding it. And so, it could be said that the Divine, in his expression of Himself, is in perpetual progress towards a more and more perfect, a more and more divine manifestation.

And in that case, each element has only to manifest, as perfectly as possible, its own law, what it should be in the whole, in order to do the utmost of what ought to be done. It is thus a conscious, an enlightened, one could almost say a disinterested, discovery of this truth of each being, which for it is the first and most important necessity.[86]

THE MOTHER

GLOSSARY

(Some of the more unfamiliar terms in this book have been defined here.)

desire-soul — the surface soul which expresses itself in our cravings, impulses, feelings, emotions, ambitions, etc.; it is distinguished from the true soul in us — the psychic being.

life — an energy of the Spirit which constitutes the link between body and mind in the human make-up; in the context of evolution, Life is what evolves out of Matter and is followed by the emergence of Mind; it is the middle term between Mind and Matter.

Overmind — the highest of the planes of consciousness below the Supermind; it is the intermediary line between the higher half of the universe of consciousness constituted of Sat, Chit, Ananda, Mahas (Existence, Consciousness, Bliss, Supermind) and the lower half of Mind, Life, Matter. It is the delegate of the Supramental Consciousness (the Truth-Consciousness) to the cosmic Ignorance (the Ignorance of oneness, the separative consciousness and the egoistic mind and life that flow from it); it is the world of the great Gods, the divine Creators in the cosmos.

psychic being — the evolving soul of the individual; whereas the psychic *essence* is present in every thing and creature, it is only in the human being that it becomes individualised and is then called the psychic *being*.

Supermind — the highest divine consciousness and force operative in the universe, also called the Truth-Consciousness because it is a principle superior to mentality and exists, acts and proceeds in the fundamental truth and unity of things and not like the mind in their appearances and phenomenal divisions.

the vital (being) — the life-force acting in impulses, desires, emotions, etc.

Yogashakti — spiritual force which is popularly associated with Kundalini, the sleeping serpent of Energy within.

REFERENCES

Passages in this book, serially numbered from 1–86, have been extracted from the following volumes of the Sri Aurobindo Birth Centenary Library (1970–73) and the Collected Works of the Mother (1972–80) published by Sri Aurobindo Ashram, Pondicherry.

For the convenience of those who have subscribed to the latest edition of Sri Aurobindo's works (The Complete Works of Sri Aurobindo), now in process of publication by Sri Aurobindo Ashram, those references are also given for the volumes already published.

Sri Aurobindo Birth Centenary Library (SABCL)

Vol.	Title
15	*Social and Political Thought*
17	*The Hour of God and Other Writings*
20	*The Synthesis of Yoga — Parts One and Two*
22	*Letters on Yoga — Part One*
23	*Letters on Yoga — Parts Two and Three*
24	*Letters on Yoga — Part Four*

Complete Works of Sri Aurobindo (CWSA)

Vol.	Title
12	*Essays Human and Divine*
23	*Synthesis of Yoga — Parts One and Two*
25	*The Human Cycle*

Collected Works of the Mother (CWM)

Vol.	Title
6	*Questions and Answers 1954*
7	*Questions and Answers 1955*
8	*Questions and Answers 1956*
9	*Questions and Answers 1957–58*
10	*On Thoughts and Aphorisms*
15	*Words of the Mother*

References are given below in an abbreviated form. The initial numeral is the serial number of the passage in this book located at the end of each passage. This is followed by the abbreviated title of the series (SABCL, CWSA, or CWM), followed by the volume number and the page number(s) where the passage occurs. For example:

1 CWM 9:112-13 indicates that passage 1 is to be found in the *Collected Works of the Mother* Volume 9 on pages 112-13.

Living Words

1	CWM 9:112-13
2	CWM 8:311

Rising Above the Subhuman

3a	SABCL 15:95
3b	CWSA 25:74
4	CWM 7:329-30
5	CWM 7:313-15

Ascension Beyond the Human

6a	SABCL 17:7-9
6b	CWSA 12:57
7	CWM 7:354-56
8	CWM 7:282-83
9	CWM 9:310-11
10	CWM 9:43-46
11	CWM 7:407-08
12a	SABCL 17:74-75

12b	CWSA 12:150-51
13	CWM 9:426-28

Desire, Pain, Pleasure and Delight

14	CWM 8:70-71
15	CWM 7:37-40
16	CWM 10:172-74
17	CWM 9:40-42
18	CWM 9:20-21
19	CWM 9:22-23

Sin, Evil and Ugliness

20	CWM 9:133-35
21	CWM 10:75-78
22	CWM 10:120-24
23	CWM 10:71-74

Light on the Path

24	CWM 7:177-78
25a	SABCL 20:63-65
25b	CWSA 23:69-71
26a	SABCL 20:51-53
26b	CWSA 23:58-59
27	CWM 8:228-29
28	CWM 7:68-69
29	CWM 7:211-14
30	CWM 9:64-65
31	CWM 7:245-46
32	CWM 7:419-21
33	CWM 9:116-19
34	CWM 10:34-35
35	CWM 6:404-05
36	CWM 8:383-86
37	CWM 9:316-17
38	CWM 15:397-98
39	CWM 8:282-83
40	CWM 6:402-03
41	CWM 9:423-26
42	CWM 8:286-88
43	CWM 6:442-45

Experiences on the Path

44	CWM 10:19-20
45	CWM 7:77-80
46	CWM 7:291-92
47	CWM 9:406-08
48	CWM 8:283-84
49	CWM 8:341-43

The Guide, Helper, Lord Divine

50a	SABCL 17:2
50b	CWSA 12:5
51	SABCL 22:168
52	CWM 9:339-40
53	SABCL 24:1626-29
54	CWM 9:29-32
55a	SABCL 20:53
55b	CWSA 23:59-60
56	CWM 8:122-23
57	CWM 10:152-54
58	CWM 9:419-21
59	CWM 8:305-06

60	CWM 7:247-48
61	CWM 8:74-79
62	CWM 10:154-56
63	CWM 8:39-40
64	CWM 10:156-59
65	CWM 8:251
66	CWM 8:121-22
67	CWM 8:301-03
68a	SABCL 17:1
68b	CWSA 12:146

The Gospel of Faith

69	SABCL 23:573
70	SABCL 23:575-76
71	CWM 8:38-39
72	CWM 6:403-04
73	CWM 9:350-52
74	SABCL 20:47
74	CWSA 23:53-54
75	CWM 7:343
76	CWM 8:23
77	SABCL 23:584-85
78	CWM 6:176-77

A New World is Born, Born

79	CWM 9:145-50
80	CWM 9:156-58
81	CWM 9:324-46
82	CWM 9:5-6
83	CWM 9:337-38
84	CWM 7:418-19
85	CWM 9:158-59
86	CWM 8:324-26

Compilations from the works of Sri Aurobindo and the Mother by the same Editor

Living Within
The Yoga Approach to Psychological Health and Growth

The Psychic Being
Soul — Its Nature, Mission and Evolution

The Hidden Forces of Life

Growing Within
The Psychology of Inner Development

Looking from Within
A Seeker's Guide to Attitudes for Mastery and Inner Growth

Powers Within

Living Words
Soul-Kindlers for the New Millennium

Our Many Selves:
Practical Yogic Psychology

Emergence of the Psychic:
Governance of Life by the Soul

The Yoga of Sleep and Dreams
The Night-School of Sadhana